LAND OF
ENCHANTMENT

Memoirs of Marian Russell
Along the Santa Fe Trail
As dictated to
Mrs. Hal Russell

Illustrated Facsimile Edition
with
New Photographs,
a New Map,
and a New Afterword
by Marc Simmons

University of New Mexico Press ● Albuquerque

International Standard Book Number 0-8263-0571-7.
International Standard Book Number (paperback) 0-8263-0805-8
Third Paperback Printing 1989

Library of Congress Cataloging in Publication Data
Russell, Marian Sloan, 1845–1937.
    Land of enchantment.

    Reprint. Originally published: Evanston, Ill.:
Branding Iron Press, 1954.
    Includes index.
    1. Santa Fe Trail.   2. Frontier and pioneer life—Southwest, New.   3. Overland journeys to the
Pacific.   4. Russell, Marian Sloan, 1845–1937.   5. Pioneers—Southwest, New—Biography.
6. Southwest, New—Biography.   I. Title.
F786.R96   1981   917.8   80-54564
ISBN 0-8263-0571-7   AACR2

MEMOIRS OF MARIAN RUSSELL

RICHARD D. RUSSELL   MARIAN SLOAN RUSSELL
    1839– 1888   1845– 1937

From a picture taken in Santa Fe, New Mexico about 1867,
soon after their wedding.

LAND OF
ENCHANTMENT

Memoirs of Marian Russell along the
Santa Fé Trail

As dictated to

MRS. HAL RUSSELL

Edited by Garnet M. Brayer

Decorations by David T. Vernon

THE BRANDING IRON PRESS
Evanston, Illinois:1954

Between the Covers ....

Down the trail. . . .

FEW OF the great overland highways of America have known
such a wealth of color and romance as that which surrounded
the Santa Fé Trail. For over four centuries the dust-gray
and muddy-red trail felt the moccasined tread of Comanches,
Apaches, Cheyennes, and Arapahoes. These soft footfalls
were replaced by the bold harsh clang of the armored con-
queror, Coronado, and by a host of Spanish explorers and
soliders seeking the gold of fabled Quivira. Black and brown-
robed priests, armed only with the cross, were followed in
turn by bearded buckskin-clad fur traders and mountain
men, by canny Indian traders, and lean, weather-beaten
drovers with great herds of long-horned cattle. There were
the tireless freighters marching alongside or driving heavily
laden, mile-long wagon trains; and eager, profit-conscious
merchants with trade goods for the Mexican villages of
New Mexico.

Over the years soldiers explored, surveyed, and protected
those who traveled on the slender wavering ribbon which
linked precariously the quiet pastoral culture of hispanic
New Mexico and the dynamic restless culture of the blos-
soming French, Spanish, and then American settlements a
thousand miles to the East. It was a colorful handful who
accepted such grave responsibility: armor-clad *conquistadores*
of imperial Spain, Mexican lancers, American dragoons,
infantry, and Negro cavalry. There were Texas militiamen,
Kansas guerrillas fresh from the farms, and Colorado volun-

xi

teers still covered with the grime of the gold and silver camps of the Rockies.

Names great and small became associated with the trail. There was "Kit" Carson, "Old" Bill Williams, "Jed" Smith, the Pattie's, and "Broken Hand" Fitzpatrick, Lelande and Becknell, Cerán St. Vrain, the brothers Bent, Alexander Barclay, Sibley, Kearney, Quantrill, and Custer. "Pilgrims," pioneers, and prospectors—tens of thousands of them— jolted over the rolling ruts past old Fort Bent to Fort Union, and through the narrow pass to the ancient adobe pueblo of Santa Fé. Others pushed past the mud villages of the Rio Grande and across mountains and desert to the gold fields of California—and ten years later to the Pike's Peak diggings. It was a trail of promise, and a trail of blood.

The rhythmical beat of the bright painted tom-toms of ten thousand red warriors blended with the earth-shaking thunder of a million buffalo, and with the tortured screech of uncounted thousands of lumbering wagon wheels bearing men and women to a new life in a new land. In the mind's eye of each was the ageless dream of freedom and opportunity. Many found what they sought. Others found only dismal failure and an unmarked grave. No one ever called it an easy life. The romance came later . . . largely in retrospect.

The story dictated in such vivid detail by Marian Sloan Russell is a unique and valuable eyewitness account by a sensitive, intelligent girl who grew to maturity on the kaleidoscopic Santa Fé Trail. "Maid Marian," as she was known by the freighters and soldiers, made five round-trip crossings of the trail before settling down to live her adult life along its deeply rutted traces.

Among her earliest memories were those of a child in a great westbound wagon train; of a children's playground in the "no man's land" between two great protective circles formed at day's end by the prairie schooners; of cool noon-day meals while weary drivers and guards caught "forty winks" stretched in the shade under the wagon beds; of the huge reddish spiders that dwelt beneath the buffalo chips that she gathered for the campfires each morning and evening on the treeless plains.

It is not only in the detailed memories, incidents, and anecdotes of life on and along the trail that Marian Russell's story makes its contribution, but in the recording of the emotions, stresses, and reactions of those who had to meet and deal promptly and decisively with each new problem and situation. Characterized by the late Earl Van Dale as "the finest trail account written by a woman—surpassing even those of Mrs. Summerhayes and Susan Magoffin," Marian Russell's finely drawn picture reveals the human side of trail and frontier life. It contains one of the very few eye-witness descriptions of Colonel Christopher "Kit" Carson at the peak of his career. No less important are the warm, intimate pictures sketched of that other leading trailsman, Captain Francis Aubry, and the energetic, almost saint-like first Bishop of Santa Fé, Jean Baptiste Lamy.

Marian Russell has made a truly significant contribution by reminding her readers that there was a second and more permanent side to the traditional picture of rugged western life. The wild terror of Indian warfare; range, land, and mining wars; vigilantes; outlaws; cheap life and quick death; wild game; disastrous winters and prolonged summer droughts were in fact a colorful façade behind which lay indomitable courage, infinite patience, steadfast integrity, and almost unbelievable self-sacrifice. Behind the temporary false front of the "Wild West" was a breed of pioneers from almost every nation in the world; men and women of almost every race, color, and creed who believed in law and order, in freedom and independence, in democracy and in God's love and forgiveness. And at the core of this pioneer foundation was the family—such a family as that of Marian Russell.

In Mrs. Hal Russell, an educated, understanding, and sympathetic daughter-in-law, Marian Russell found an able amanuensis. Hour upon hour, day after day, and month after month the aging pioneer dictated—her eyes aglow as each detail and incident reminded her of another and yet another vivid memory. Faithfully, and almost tirelessly, her schoolteacher daughter-in-law wrote, read back, and corrected the account. It is published here as it was dictated . . . a monument to the pioneering spirit of the men and their women who carved a fruitful land and life from a raw wilderness.

Within sight of the broad deep ruts of the trail which stretched its thin tentacles far to the East as well as to the West, Marian Russell lived a long and useful life. She died in 1936 in Trinidad, Colorado, at ninety-two years of age, after being struck down by an automobile. At long last she was free to travel for all eternity in her great wagon with the billowing white canvas over the long, long trails of her Enchanted Land.

CHAPTER ONE

The Old Northwest

IT IS my desire that these memoirs may help preserve to posterity the truth and the warmth of an unforgettable period in American history; the stirring decades in which sturdy pioneers blazed trails across a strange and wondrous land of prairies, plains and mountains.

Life has dealt me adventure with a lavish hand and yet the way stretches very fair behind me. It is the brightness, not the darkness that I see as I look backward.

It is in the little incidents of life that the interest of existence really lies, not in just the grand results. For that reason I hope the reader will bear with me if I stray at times from the main thread of my story to linger over some cherished personal remembrance. Dear to me is the memory of that cloud of dust that swirled away behind a lumbering herd of buffalo, of curlews dipping in a moist meadow, of cows in a line ambling to the milking shed, of trips across the Great Plains in a covered wagon, of my honey-moon in little Camp Nickols on the Santa Fé Trail, of Colonel "Kit" Carson and Colonel Francis X. Aubry. I like to remember how the Santa Fé Trail traffic flowed like a river through Santa Fé's great arched gateway.

I am the third and last child of William and Eliza St. Clair Sloan, who were of Scottish ancestry. They named me after Lady Marian Wallace whose tragic story touched my mother's heart. I was born in Peoria, Illinois, on January 26, 1845. The first child of my parents' union died in infancy. The next, my brother, William, lived to manhood and shared with me many of the incidents of which I write.

My father, an army surgeon in the Mexican War, was killed at the Battle of Monterey. He passed from my life at such an early age that I have no remembrance of him. An old daguerreotype shows him in a gaily-flowered waist coat, with long straight dark hair and serious eyes like brother Will's.

I became so familiar with my mother's face as it was in later years that her earlier image evades me. She was a small very dark but lovely woman. She was courageous, educated and cultured. One hundred years ago educational advantages were difficult for a boy and girl to obtain, yet mother managed to give both Will and me educations far beyond the average.

At times I seem to see her standing by a flickering campfire in a flounced gingham dress and a great sunbonnet. Behind her looms the great bulk of a covered wagon. I think I can hear her singing,

Flow gently sweet Afton,
Among thy green braes.

From the shadowy background of infancy come pictures of amazing clarity. Across a room of immaculate cleanliness I send my toddling feet. There is white Chinese matting on the floor, and in a corner a stand table, the top of which I cannot reach, bearing a big conch shell and a vase of flowers. There are guests: A man with black side-burns who has carefully parted his long coat tails before sitting down; a woman whose silken skirts billow softly as she sweeps across the Chinese matting. She wears black silk halfhanders and carrys a large fan. Her blue eyes stare solemnly at me from above the widespread fan. This is my first remembrance of our home in St. Louis, Missouri.

Out of childhood come other memories: The vegetable garden behind the house in which we later lived in St. Louis was a wild unexplored jungle in which strange

2

beasts might be found hidden among the currants and cabbage. Once a wild Indian with a feather in his hair arose with blood-curdling war whoops from among the tomato vines. On closer inspection the savage turned out to be brother Will, yet the vegetable garden remained a wild jungle.

My step-father, whose name was Mahoney, killed a snake in my jungle garden. It was a rattle-snake with eleven rattles. I stood with my hand in my mother's and, from a safe distance, looked at the dead snake. Suddenly, the dead snake opened its mouth wide and out jumped a big green toad. For a moment, it stood blinking its eyes at us, then went hopping off amid the cabbages. I think perhaps that the memory of the rattle-snake and the hop-toad has always inclined me to believe a wee bit in ghosts and goblins.

The world! What a vast mysterious place it seemed to my childlike eyes! What a trackless continent the vegetable garden! What marvelous explorations I could make in our attic!

Then there was the street; the street that stretched long and dim from our doorstep. It led to a strange unknown world, of that I was certain. Through the long summer days it beckoned and so at last I did follow. Soon the street became dreadful and unfamiliar, and an almighty and devastating sadness descended upon me. I wanted my mother. But all around me stretched St. Louis, a dreadful and strange St. Louis. I was tired. I was sick and I wanted my mother. I climbed some white wooden steps to where a door stood hospitably open. A woman's sweet voice bade me enter. I would not talk to the woman. How could she know of a street that invited and enticed small children away from their mother? She gave me bread and milk in a blue bowl and a gray kitten came and softly rubbed against me. I was comforted.

There were no radio patrol cars in St. Louis in 1848. When three year old children strayed away from their mothers they depended upon an old negro to find them. Soon an old negro came along that now frightening street.

3

He was ringing a bell as he walked, and his soft voice was calling, "Little while chile lost. Have you seen a three year old chile in a blue pinafore? Little Marian Sloan is lost from her mother." So, I was found and, fast asleep, I was carried home to my mother. I only remember cradling my head on a warm black neck before slumber engulfed me.

I remember sitting in a great room. The air was close and heavy from the breathing of a large audience. I had leaned my head against mother sleepily when the curtain before us suddenly went up with a clatter. Little Tom Thumb, all dressed in red velvet and golden tassels, drove out on the stage a team of tiny Shetland ponies hitched to a little buggy. The audience laughed and clapped. The tiny ponies danced as little Tom stood up in the buggy, removed his top hat and bowed to us. Then a man came and stood at the edge of the stage and talked for awhile. He said that the buggy and ponies had been given to Tom Thumb by Queen Victoria.

I often had to be reminded to say my prayers, but Will never had to be reminded. I can see him kneeling by his bed that was always across the room from mother's and mine, his thin brown neck rising above the collar of his outing flannel night shirt. Once I laughed at the sight of the brown soles of his bare feet sticking out behind him. I laughed but mother's glance reproved me. Will never noticed. His piping voice had begun the child's prayer, "Now I lay me . . ." He hesitated one night when he had finished and, after a moment added a bit defiantly,"Please God, I want some day to see your face. Dear God, I will be a good boy."

I turned shocked eyes upon my mother. She dropped my long hair she was braiding and crossed the room to kneel at Will's side. I seem to see them kneeling there. I see their shadows flickering on the wall. I hear a child's voice saying, "Please God, I want to see your face."

So they come, these childhood memories. They are fragmentary and disconnected, life's loose beads with no straight string running through them.

4

Mother had remarried when I was but three years old and the memory of my step-father's kindness colors many of my childhood memories. He was a tall man, an Irishman with a red face and broad shoulders. I do not know why I was not taught to call him "father." To me he was always Mr. Mahoney. He carried himself with an erect military bearing and seemed to know all there was to know about Indians. The tales he told of the red men! He had an eager boyish laugh and fine even white teeth that gleamed when he laughed. I remember that he would play the banjo and sing Irish ballads with a good strong voice with a rollicking note in it.

He seemed to love to be near mother. They made a nice looking couple though mother could stand under his outstretched arm, she was so small. He was tall, yellow-haired and florid. She was short, dark and utterly lovely.

I do wish you could have seen mother in her hooped skirts and snowy pantalettes. Her hoops were never over-large, but the pantalettes were so glistening, stiff-starched and lace trimmed. They were embroidered and ruffled and removable. She took them off like a pair of stockings. She anchored them above her knees with elastic and was always changing them.

Mother parted her black hair in the middle and combed it smoothly back to a bun that she anchored with bone hairpins. No matter how smoothly she combed that black hair tendrils of it always came loose and flew about. Her eyes were large and Madonna-like 'neath the heavy, parted hair. When she became excited her face flushed like a rose leaf.

I remember sitting on the floor holding Mr. Mahoney's new boots in my lap. My feet, shod in black sandals, were stretched out before me. Somewhere I had seen a picture of a mouse running out of a hole in the toe of a boot. So with mother's forbidden scissors I cut a small hole in the toe of Mr. Mahoney's new boot. Outraged, mother quickly lifted her hand against me. But Mr. Mahoney took me from her. He laughed as he held my face hard against his own. To my very angry mother he said, "Of

5

boots there are many, but I have only one dear little daughter." I loved Mr. Mahoney.

In 1849, Mr. Mahoney was appointed custodian of Fort Snelling and Prairie du Chien, military outposts on the upper Mississippi.[1] Garrisons of soldiers were stationed there to guard against Indian outbreaks. Mr. Mahoney was an experienced scout and knew the way of the red man.

We packed our belongings and took passage on a funny little stern-wheeler that churned up the muddy waters, leaving a foamy, ivory colored trail in its wake. It was a bit like a sawmill in full operation moving off up the river. Then, too, there was a charm and a mystery about the river. We were enroute to a new home in the great northwest. Everything along the Father of Waters was different from our life in St. Louis.

On the western side of that great yellow river rippled the silvery prairies, with their danger from Indians and wild buffalo. We saw herds of buffalo grazing. Little towns perched on the bluffs above the eastern bank of the great river. There were tall trees and vines whose tendrils hung down into the murky water. All the little towns were on the eastern bank. The western bank was left to the buffalo and to the Indians.

We passed many islands and wondered how the pilot of the threshing little stern-wheeler found his way through them. In places there were so many islands that we had the illusion we were sailing through a series of many little lakes.

Sometimes we passed under angry red bluffs that frowned down at us. One such tall prominence was named "The Maiden's Leap," and mother told us the story of the Indian girl who had thrown herself from the precipice when her lover had proved unfaithful. Mr. Mahoney said that he hoped her lover was a Sioux and not a dirty Chippewa. Mr. Mahoney did not approve of the Chippewas.

In later years I was to learn the full legend. A hundred years before, an Indian girl named Winona, of the tribe of

6

Wapasha, fell in love with a young Indian hunter. Her love was returned but her parents wanted her to marry another warrior who had signally distinguished himself in battle against the hated Chippewas.

When the fateful day came that Winona was to be married to the man of her parent's choice, she ascended to the summit of the high red bluff and, in a clear ringing voice, upbraided her father for being cruel to her lover and driving him alone into the forest. She then lifted her hands to the sky above her and began singing a plaintive song to her lover. When the song was finished she threw herself into the river.

Standing that day on the deck of the little stern-wheeler I saw in imagination the slender Indian girl hurtling down into the water. I leaned far over trying to see the bottom, but the water was yellow and muddy. Poor little Winona!

At last we anchored beneath a high cut bank. On the top stood Fort Snelling. There was a tall round tower in the center of the parade ground and from it a sentry on duty scanned the countryside for roving bands of Indians.

Across the river from Fort Snelling were Indian encampments of Sioux and Chippewas. One could not help noticing how much cleaner were the Sioux than the Chippewas. Even from across the river the gaily colored blankets of the Sioux contrasted oddly with the dirty, bedraggled ones of the Chippewas.

Once the Sioux came scampering to the gates of the fort for protection. Hard on their heels were the screaming Chippewas. In an instant all became bustle and confusion. A detachment of soldiers marched out between the warring factions. The Chippewas muttered and grumbled. The Sioux brought out a big peace pipe. There was some smoking and grunting. At last the laughing soldiers trooped back into the fort and the Indians returned to their camp across the river. The "battle" was over.

Many distinguished officers had been in charge at Fort Snelling. Zachary Taylor had been in command there twenty years before. He had four beautiful daughters, one of whom was my mother's friend. She married Jefferson Davis.

7

Dred Scott, too, had lived at Fort Snelling. He was a negro slave belonging to Dr. Emerson, an army surgeon. Dr. Emerson also owned a mulatto girl with a skin like yellow satin. Dred married this pretty negress at Fort Snelling in 1836. Later when Dr. Emerson was transferred to St. Louis he sold Dred and his wife "down the river." It was then that Dred brought suit for his freedom. The case was carried to the Supreme Court and resulted in the infamous Dred Scott Decision.

Prairie du Chien was not far south of Fort Snelling. Many of the officers were stationed at Prairie du Chien. While we lived at Fort Snelling we made many trips down to Prairie du Chien in mule-drawn covered wagons. On one such occasion we passed through the village of the French voyageurs. Tall houses edged streets so narrow that they seemed hardly wide enough for our great wagons. Women with bright black eyes and shawls over their heads called to us from open doorways. The voyageurs were famous hunters, trappers, fishermen and boatmen. Often at Fort Snelling we would see them coming up the river in keel boats. Each boat had four tiny sails and a cabin amidships.

One such voyageur was Antony, a gnome-like fellow with a face like a withered apple. Never did he come to Fort Snelling but that he found Will and me waiting for him. He had a pleasant sun-burnt face and a little choppy mustache beneath which his teeth shone when he smiled. Many were the tales he told of murderous French priests and an ancient folk he called "the Druids." Druid legends had the Indian stories beat. The Druids lived in haunted woods and though they looked like people they were not human. They had long tails and they lived in the heart of the forest trees. If one was unfortunate enough to cut a bough from a tree in which a Druid made his home, that person would either die suddenly or become crippled in one of his limbs.

Old Antony told us that the cotton wood trees that grew along the river had a spirit that was a bit like a ghost, and that Will and I must learn to respect that

8

spirit. The ghost of the cottonwood tree had helped the voyageurs in all of their undertakings. When the Mississippi, swollen by spring rains, carried away part of its bank and a tall tree fell into the current, the spirit of the tree could be heard crying while its roots clung to the soil and its trunk lay down in the water.

We made many trips up and down the river while we lived at Fort Snelling. Once we camped at the Falls of St. Anthony and Mr. Mahoney caught a string of catfish as yellowish-black as the waters of the river. He also caught a sturgeon, with a three-cornered head like a cocked hat, and its mouth on the under side. It looked like a mud-plow. While Mr. Mahoney was fishing we saw a caribou come down to the river's edge for a drink, and an old buffalo swam out to a little island and lay clumsily down to rest.

Once mother and I went down to St. Paul to do a little shopping. St. Paul had no paved streets in '49 and I remember how we waded through the mud from one store to another, and how mother held up her long purple dress and how mud got all over her cloth shoes that were buttoned down at the sides.

As I write I again experience the thrill that was mine when we moved away from Fort Snelling. Orders had come from headquarters that both Fort Snelling and Prairie du Chien were to be abandoned. All day long troops had been leaving. The blooded horses from the military stables had been loaded on a stern-wheeler.

In our quarters, trunks, bags and boxes stood open for mother was packing. She sorted, packed and eliminated. This article or that one she would tuck into a box or bag, while another she would toss upon a refuse heap in the corner. Here was a game of leave and take that delighted my soul beyond measure. Into the kitchen I marched, gathered up my rag doll and my little tin dipper. The dipper I put into an open box, the rag doll I threw into a tub of water. My little rag doll that had slept with me all the time we lived at Fort Snelling! She eddied around a bit, gazing at me all the while with soulful, shoe-button eyes. Filled with compunction and sorrow, I backed slowly from the room, watching spell-bound the little painted face on the water.

I stood then with Mr. Mahoney on the big front steps of the fort. Across the river the Sioux were getting ready to leave; their teepees were coming down. The Chippewas had already gone. I saw Mr. Mahoney fit the key in the lock of the fort. That key must have been a foot long and folded in the middle like a jack-knife. When the door was locked, he picked me up and set me on his shoulder. I felt the cool, sweet wind on my face and from my high vantage point I looked up at the great round tower. For the first time no sentry stood there.

Thus Fort Snelling, Prairie du Chien and the first chapter of my life closed together.

CHAPTER TWO

On the Santa Fé Trail

MR. MAHONEY was killed by the Indians while he was out on a scouting expedition. Of his death I have nothing but a hazy recollection. I remember mostly my mother and how, when the news came, she leaned against the wall for support, one hand clutching at her throat as if she were choking. I remember the horror in her eyes. It did not occur to me that I would never see my Mr. Mahoney again; never see his great gnarled hands and that shock of yellowish hair. They did not tell me how out on the prairies there had been an Indian waiting in ambush, or how before he died he had asked that his love be given to Eliza and little Marian. When I think of my step-father I think of a man with sunshine in his face and a rollicking sound in his voice.

After my step-father's death, mother, Will and I waited two long years in Kansas City. We waited for Grandfather Sloan to come and get us. He and his two sons had gone out to California several years before. Many were the golden tales they had written of California where gold might be had for the asking. Once they had written how our great aunt, Mary Rice, had washed out three-thousand dollars worth of gold with her own hands at a place called Sutter's Fort. Now Grandfather Sloan had written that he was coming and would take us back to California with him. We might wash out much gold if we cared to. Mother was anxious to go. She was lonely and the interest she had had in life seemed waning. So we waited for grandfather to come for us; but we waited in vain. That was the year of the cholera epidemic, and grandfather and both of his sons died with it and were buried in far away California. The news reached us slowly. Wagon trains were often a year making the trip from California.

During this waiting period I attended a Catholic primary school of the Sacred Heart in Kansas City. It pleased me mightily to learn that the small black curlicues in my primer really meant something. It was wonderful to make letters on a slate that was bound all around with bright red wool and to rub the letters out with a small yellow sponge that the teacher said had grown down on the bottom of the ocean. I wore clean little white pinafores with a pocket for my handkerchief. The Sisters moved quietly among us and sometimes our lessons were from the Bible. They told us how the pearls of the sea, the flowers from the garden, and the stars in the Heavens had been woven into a garland; a garland called the Bible. They taught us to think of the Bible as a light shining in darkness. They taught us to enjoy the faultless rhythm of the Psalms. Yet we were so young. Only children of six and seven attended the primary school of the Sacred Heart in Kansas City.

When school closed in the spring of 1852, mother decided that we would go to California anyway. So we left Kansas City and moved to Fort Leavenworth where immigrant trains were wont to assemble in preparation for the trip westward. Fort Leavenworth was a little city of tents and covered wagons encamped on the edge of the prairies. Wagon trains from the east and west were arriving daily.

Mother's friend and ardent admirer was Francis Xavier Aubry, a famous wagon master.[2] He was a young man some where in his late twenties. I remember his young piercing eyes and his boundless energy. He was a virile man, with a deep voice that was as resonant as a fog horn. Mother had planned that we were to take passage in Captain Aubry's train, for the Indians were bad along the Santa Fé Trail and she had great confidence in him.

Captain Aubry's train was encamped at Fort Leavenworth waiting until more wagons arrived westward bound. The more wagons the greater safety from attack by the Indians. At last a big government train pulled in from the east and Captain Aubry made plans for an early departure.

Passengers on the government train included three young men. Two were army officers enroute to Fort Union. The third was a graduate doctor from West Point. These young men offered mother, Will and me transportation as far as Fort Union if mother would prepare their meals enroute for them. Mother gladly agreed for transportation from Fort Leavenworth to Santa Fé, New Mexico, in 1852, was $250.00 and, of course, there was also half fare for the children. She saved $500 by cooking for the young men, besides which they furnished the provisions.

During our enforced wait at Fort Leavenworth, Will and I had become acquainted with Captain Aubry. He was our very good friend. We took our childish woes to him for solace, visiting him in his great covered wagon. He was not pleased because Will was thin and pale looking. It worried him because Will spent so much time reading. Before we reached Santa Fé he said he would make a great hunter and trapper out of Will. He told us that Indians were as thick as hops along the trail, but that we did not need to be afraid of them. Gradually, however, we came to know that every one in the waiting wagon-train was torn between joy at making the great overland trip and terror of the Indians. Tales of frightful Indian atrocities were told without number.

A will-o'-the-wisp was the Santa Fé Trail, an ancient route and one of the longest in history. It led from our eastern seaboard to the waters of the blue Pacific. If we could but measure it by the tears and the smiles it has known we would never be able to trace its way through American history. Along the trail the Indians slaughtered and burned. The bones of their victims oft whitened along the trail. The yucca shook out white bells along the

13

way. Northern lights beckoned. And daily the covered wagons left Fort Leavenworth over the broad, rutted road stretching westward as far as the eye could see.

The dread cholera was raging in Fort Leavenworth the day our white-hooded wagons set sail on the western prairies. Our little city of tents dissolved like snow in a summer sun. Captain Aubry broke camp first; his great wagon swayed out onto the trail. We heard his powerful voice calling orders to follow. Wagon after wagon rolled onward and it was not until the last of Captain Aubry's wagons was well on the trail that the first of the government wagons followed. Our leader drove four mouse-colored mules which scampered like frisky dogs and tried to run away.

The timid were always frightened, but most of the people felt safe for the train now numbered more than 500 wagons. Tar barrels were burning in the streets of Fort Leavenworth to ward off the cholera, and clouds of black smoke drifted over us as we pulled out.

I remember so clearly the beauty of the earth, and how, as we bore westward, the deer and the antelope bounded away from us. There were miles and miles of buffalo grass, blue lagoons and blood-red sunsets and, once in a while, a little sod house on the lonely prairie— home of some hunter or trapper.

We were a bit over two months reaching Fort Union in New Mexico. It was an eventful two months. Most of the wagons were laden with supplies for the fort or for Santa Fé. The freight rate to Santa Fé was $10.00 per hundred pounds. Teamsters and drivers were paid $25.00 per month plus rations. This first trip we made over what is now known as the Cimarron Cut-off. It left the Arkansas River west of Fort Dodge, Kansas, and bore in a south-westernly direction until it reached the Cimarron River in what is now Oklahoma. Our long caravan, loaded with heavy, valuable merchandise, traveled slowly. Sometimes we were alarmed by the Indians, threatened by storms, and always it seemed we suffered for want of water.

Minute impressions flash before me; the sun-bonnetted women, the woolen-trousered men, little mother in her flounced gingham, brother Will walking in long strides by our driver, voices of the lonely and homeless singing around blazing campfires. Because I was one of the youngest, I may today be the only one left of that band to tell of the old, old, trail that, like a rainbow, led us westward.

Our trail often led among herds of buffalo so numerous that at times we were half afraid. The vast open country that is gone from us forever rippled like a silver sea in the sunshine. Running across that sea of grass were the buffalo trails; narrow paths worn deep into the earth. They were seldom more than eight inches across, and always ran north and south. A buffalo is a wise animal and knows instinctively that water flows eastward away from the Rocky Mountains and that the nearest way to running water was always north or south. Scattered along the buffalo trails were the buffalo wallows, small lagoons of rain water. They were like turquoise beads strung on a dark-brown string. The buffalo wallows, they told us, were made by buffalo bulls fighting. They would put their heads together and slowly walk round and round making a depression that caught the rain water.

Frightening thunder storms came up suddenly. They would sweep over us, and away they would go as suddenly as they had come. When the sky would darken and the forked lightning sent the thunder rolling, the drivers would wheel the wagons so that the mules' backs were to the storm. The men who had been walking would seek shelter with the women and children inside the wagons. The prairies would darken and then would come a mighty clap of thunder and a sheet of drenching water would fall from the skies upon us. A fine white mist would come through the tightened canvas and soon small pearl beads would glisten in mother's hair. So we would sit through wind, water, thunder, and lightning. Then, as suddenly as it had come, the storm would pass away. We would emerge then from the wagons to stretch our cramped limbs and to see the golden sun shining through the scattered clouds. Always we saw our storm, a tattered beggar, limping off across the distant hills. Looking back now it seems to me that we had a thunder storm almost every day.

There, too, was the wonder of the skies. Morning after morning we watched the great land flare into beauty. Evening after evening we watched the prairie sun go down in its glory, and then watched the white stars shine in the night above us.

There was the desert mirage, a will-'o-the-wisp that beckoned and taunted. Sometimes it would look like a party of mounted Indians and the women would cry and begin counting their children. Sometimes it would look like a tall castle set among the trees, or a blue lake with waves lapping white sand. It danced ever before us through the hot hours and only disappeared at sunset.

There were also the rainbows. If I had ever seen rain bows before I had forgotten them. The rainbows I love to remember are the ones that spanned the old trail. One evening a great rainbow flashed through the sun-lit rain. It was so big and so lovely! I called out to mother who stood on the wagon tongue searching inside for some cooking utensil. Turning and facing the red splendor, she cried out in delight. Will, who was busy kindling a cooking fire said with some eloquence, "There is always a pot of gold at the end of each rainbow."

"Mother, is it really true about the pot of gold?" I asked, awed by Will's knowledge. She sat perched on the end gate of the great wagon, her eyes on the red splendor. "They say so, child," was her only answer.

"Why the end of the rainbow is just beyond the little green hill before us. If Will will come with me, we will bring the pot of gold to you." I was delighted.

Mother's eyes came to rest on her small daughter. She smiled as she answered, "The end of the rainbow is always much farther away than it seems, dear. If you climb the green hill the rainbow will still be before you. I think, perhaps, that it rests in California at a place called Sutter's Fort. We can only follow the rainbow and hope that it leads to fame and fortune."

16

For years I thought that the end of the rainbow was in California.

There were other things that lifted our eyes to the sky. There was the gray day when we saw the wild geese flying southward. Honking, the huge, graceful birds streamed overhead. The sky was full of beating wings. Even today it seems that I can see them sailing down the vast corridors of the clouds.

The man who drove our wagon was called Pierre. He was a swarthy Frenchman and reminded Will and me so much of old Antony that we were disappointed when we discovered that not one tale could he relate. He knew nothing of Druids, ghosts, elfins or goblins. Yet Antony's little black eyes peered out above the same choppy mustache. We decided at last that Pierre's education had been sadly neglected, and we tried to tell him what we knew about things occult and mysterious. He never laughed at us, but once his eyes widened and he said, "Who in hell told you that?"

Pierre almost always walked. Yet at times he sat swinging his booted feet over the dashboard—perilously close to the brown mule's swinging hips. Sometimes he sang or talked in French to the mules, or he conversed with mother in broken English. His limp black hat turned straight up in front. His blue shirt was dotted thickly with little white stars. His dark eyes were like hawk's eyes and his nose was like a beak. The tobacco he smoked smelled to high heaven. Our Pierre was a kindly man and one of the Government's most trusted drivers.

Our wagon was packed with boxes and bales of merchandise for Fort Union. Only the high spring seat was left for mother, Will and me. Back of the freight and on top of the packed merchandise was our bedding and camp equipment. There was a place in back among the bedding where one might rest as the wagon rolled onward. I always got sleepy and climbed back for my nap in spite of the bumps and shakes of the wagon.

Mules draw a wagon a bit more gently than horses, but oxen are best of all. 'Tis true that they walk slowly

17

but there is a rhythm in their walking that sways the great wagons gently.

Our food and cooking things were kept in a great box at the rear of the wagon, a bit like the chuck boxes of later day cow camps. Two blackened kettles and a water pail hung from the running gear of the wagon.

Mother usually sat erect on the spring seat, her face rosy in the depth of her bonnet; she burned easily. Frequently she knitted as the wagon bumped along, and often as meal and camp time drew near she sat there and peeled potatoes.

Will usually walked with Pierre, and as the days passed he seemed more hardy. He tanned in the prairie sun and there seemed boundless energy in his slender body. It was his chore to build the little cooking fires for mother; but as soon as he was free he would disappear to be with Captain Aubry.

I was seven on this trip in 1852 across the prairies, and I could not keep up with Will and Pierre by the wagon. Often, when I got tired of sitting on the hard spring seat by mother, I would crawl back among the blankets where I would play with my doll or fall asleep.

Each noon we would halt for a brief hour's rest. The lunch that we ate was a cold one. The mules fed on the crisp buffalo grass while the drivers rested. After the noon rest, we would go on again until the sun was low in the West. Then the outriders would locate the night resting place and we would stop with our wagons spread out in a great circle.

As I write scenes of the old trail come flooding back to me: Places where the earth was like a Persian rug, the lavender, red and yellow wild flowers mingling with the silvery green prairie grass. There were places where we saw wild turkeys among the cottonwood trees, and where the wild grapevines ran riot. Always there were buffalo. Sometimes we saw them walking slowly in single file along their narrow paths on the way to some distant water hole. The buffalo are gone now; gone, too, the sea of grass. When the railroads came the old trail was neglected. Weeds sprang up along its rutted way. The old trail, the long trail over which once flowed the commerce of a nation, lives now only in the memory of a few old hearts. It lives there like a lovely, oft repeated dream.

I can see the tired drivers at noonday lying under the shade of the wagons, their hats covering their faces as they slept. I can see the tired sweaty mules rolling over and over in the grass delighted to be free from the heavy wagons.

Babies were born as our wagons lumbered westward. Death sometimes came and the graves that we made we tried to obliterate by driving the wagon wheels over them. Graves must be hidden from the Indians. Bodies must not be desecrated. What the old grass grown ruts could tell! There was the little Catholic Sister on her way to Santa Fé who was simply frightened to death one day by the Indians. They buried her in a deep old rut made by the wagons. Next morning the great caravan passed over where she lay, free from fear, clasping her crucifix.

Each night there were two great circles of wagons. Captain Aubry's train encamped a half mile beyond the government's. Inside those great circles the mules were turned after grazing, for ropes were stretched between the wagons and thus a circular corral made. Inside the corral were the cooking fires, one for each wagon. After the evening meal we would gather around the little fires. The men would tell stories of the strange new land before us, tales of gold and of Indians. The women would sit with their long skirts drawn up over a sleeping child on their laps. Overhead brooded the night sky, the little camp fires flickered, and behind us loomed the dark hulks of the covered wagons.

On one night when the wind was blowing Captain Aubry came to help us with our tent. He drove the tent stakes deeper into the ground. Sparks were flying from the cooking fire that mother was endeavoring to keep ever so small. She stamped at the sparks with her little brogans. She had laid her sunbonnet aside and tendrils of her soft dark hair were blowing across her face. Captain Aubry and mother were friends of long standing, although I do not know when their friendship first started. I remember that he called her "Eliza," speaking her name slowly as if he loved saying it. Sometimes he would call her "Lizzie" and then mother would turn on him fiercely for she did not like the name "Lizzie." When mother would turn upon him, the laughter would leap up in the Captain's eyes, and watching him I always wanted to laugh, too.

On this windy night tired Will lay sleeping close by the fire where the sparks were flying. Will always walked more than he should and at night was often so tired that he could not play with the other children.

The night wind whistled among the tents, and Captain Aubry came and took me and held me on his lap. I felt the great, black night closing down upon us and heard the voice of the night wind as it swept across the turbulent prairies. The world stretched away into infinity. It was big, and black, and terrible. I shivered in the Captain's arms thinking that only in the circle of the firelight that flickered on mother's face was there warmth and comfort and home.

Between the two night circles formed by the wagons was a bit of no-man's land which the children used as a playground. The ball games that went on there! The games of leap-frog and dare base. One night I lingered long alone in little no-man's land to gather a species of white poppy that bloomed only at night. To me those prairie poppies were a fascination, blooming only when the evening shadows fell. So I lingered long in no-man's land filling my arms with their white fragrance. Above me glowed the lights of Captain Aubry's train. Below me the lights of the government train. I saw how when the lanterns were lighted inside the tents, they turned the tents into Japanese lanterns. The night wind brought to me the sound of voices and laughter. Then I saw little mother standing outside the big lighted circle. She called to me, "Mar-re-an," and there was an anxious note in her voice.

While most of the drivers slept under the wagons, the women and children slept inside the wagons or in tents. Each night we pitched the tent close to the wagon and it spread its dark wings over the three of us. It was easy to hear Pierre snoring outside. Our bed on the matted grass was comfortable, but sometimes in the night I would awaken to hear the coyote's eerie cry in the darkness. I would creep close to mother and shiver. Sometimes one of the mules would start a great braying, and others would take it up making the night hideous.

Sometimes far away we heard the war whoop of the Indians. Two men stood on guard each night, rifles in hand. They circled and recircled the big corral never slackening vigilance. Every precaution was taken so that we would not be surprised by the Indians.

One evening when Will cried with the earache, Captain Aubry stayed and blew tobacco smoke in his ear until the pain lessened. What the healing qualities of tobacco smoke were I do not know, perhaps the nicotine was a sedative. Perhaps we just thought that anything Captain Aubry did was magical! I remember how he made a willow whistle for Will, music loving Will. Soon from that willow whistle came strange sounds and merry tunes. Slender little Will, his trousers hanging from narrow hips; his eyes glowing, while from that crude little whistle came the sound of wind rushing over the prairies, the sound of birds calling from the tree tops. All the music from the pipes of Pan from one little willow whistle.

Captain Aubry taught us many things on our long voyage across the Plains. If Will were here he would remember more, for it was to Will that the Captain gave freely. Sometimes at the end of a journey it is well to look back at the path followed and to ask ourselves if there is not some lesson of hope or encouragement to be drawn from our record. Just now I keep thinking that surely somewhere there is a trail for Captain Aubry to follow, a trail that leads onward across a boundless frontier.

Each morning we awoke rested, and the camp was astir at daybreak. Men began rolling out from under the wagons. They stood up in the cold morning air to stretch their arms lustily and to rub the sleep from their eyes. Soon breakfast fires were burning and the men were catching and harnessing the mules. Through partially closed tent flaps and wagon curtains women could be seen slipping their dresses on over their heads as they sat among blankets. Children cried at being forced out from under warm covers. I found it hard to button all the buttons that ran up and down the back of my dress. Why couldn't they have been put in front where I could get at them? Will sometimes helped me, for mother was busy cooking for her boarders who always stood around looking hungry and helpless. The West Point lad was sometimes helpful but the two army officers were awkward and seemed always stumbling over a tent stake or guy rope. The West Pointer said it was a good thing he had medical training to help them heal their bruises.

Dressed and out in the sunshine we were all happy. There stretched out before us was a new-coined day, a fresh-minted world under a glorious turquoise sky. Sunbonnets bobbed merrily over cooking fires, on the air a smell of coffee. Packing was done swiftly and the mules hitched to the wagons. Then the children were counted and loaded. A swift glance about to see that nothing was left behind and we were off for another day on the trail. Drivers were calling, "Get up there! Come along, boys!" Bull whips were cracking and all about the heavy wagons began groaning. The mules leaned into the collar and the great wheels began a steady creaking. Turn where we would, flocks of prairie chicken rose and went sailing across the open country. Antelope stopped, stood still, and looked fearlessly at us.

It was strange about the prairies at dawn, they were all sepia and silver; at noon they were like molten metal, and in the evening they flared into unbelievable beauty —long streamers of red and gold were flung out across them. The sky had an unearthly radiance. Sunset on the prairie! It was haunting, unearthly and lovely.

22

Our two wagon trains had a herd of about two hundred loose horses. These horses were being taken to the post at Fort Union as saddle horses for the soldiers, and always brought up the rear of the caravan. The outriders drove them slowly that they might graze as they traveled. They were held at night outside the circle of wagons and careful night herd was kept over them. Our herd of horses was led by a lovely white stallion that belonged to Captain Sturgis of the army.

After we had been a few weeks on the trail we reached a place in Kansas called Pawnee Rock, the place of a bloody massacre a few years before. Extra precaution was taken that night, and a double sentry placed over the horse herd. During the night we were rudely awakened by the sound of Indian war whoops close at hand. From somewhere outside came the shrill screaming of the Sturgis stallion. The mules in the enclosure—mules hated Indians—were running and braying. Something struck our tent, and it came down upon us. All was bedlam, darkness and confusion. We climbed in the wagon for the mules were running like mad in the enclosure.

When morning broke our horse herd was gone—a herd of two hundred army horses. The Indians had stampeded them and driven them off in the darkness. Captain Aubry would not go on to Fort Union without the assignment of horses, so we went into camp at Pawnee Rock and waited two weeks while the out-riders went back to Fort Leavenworth to buy up more horses. Each day as we waited we were visited by roving bands of Indians. However, we were a large train and they seemed afraid to open hostilities.

The camp at Pawnee Rock gave Will and me much pleasure. Captain Aubry gave a lesson each day on the unpredictability of the Indian race. "Have eyes in the back of your head," he once stated, "and keep all your eyes open at night and day. See that big buck yonder. His face is as inexpressive as a hotel platter, but watch him. He will steal the hair from your head if you're not careful."

23

Finally the riders returned driving before them another herd of horses and we began to make preparations for departure the following morning. After leaving Pawnee Rock the fear of the Indians was with us day and night and we saw more and more of them. They seemed as thick by the trail as the buffalo, and when we reached Fort Mackey on the Arkansas River,[3] we breathed a breath of relief. It was nice to have the protection of soldiers for one night at least.

The camp at Fort Mackey lingers as a pleasant memory. Mother had given Will and me a small piece of money that we might spend as we liked at the commissary at Fort Mackey. It was with visions of red and white candy in our minds that we arose early and went to the commissary. It must have been early for I remember it was not quite light when we crept from our tent. The commissary was not open so we decided to go and visit Captain Aubry. He was up and sitting on the tongue of his wagon. He was attired in a gray flannel shirt, high top boots and a big black hat. I think in those days most western men wore big black hats; perhaps they didn't make any other color. No one in Captain Aubry's train seemed to be stirring so we sat down in the dawn and had a good visit.

The Captain seemed uneasy about us and said that we must never leave the train alone to go even a little way. He warned us that we were never again to leave the protection of the wagons, and never again were the children to be permitted to play in no-man's land. There were too many Indians and all seemed sullen, treacherous and ready to go on the war path. We promised the Captain we would not wander. He went with us to the commissary, added licorice to the red and white candy, and walked with us back to where mother waited breakfast for us.

At Fort Mackey the teamsters all seemed to do a bit of trading with the Indians. One old Indian, his ugly face painted with vermillion, traded something for a small mirror. He seemed delighted with his reflection. He would

24

gaze at himself for a while and then holding it behind him would stand and twist his face in a new kind of grimace, and then peer again at his reflection.

Some articles of real value the Indians would dispose of cheaply, while others of relatively small worth they would refuse to dispose of at any price. They had implicit faith in various charms which they thought would prevent their being killed by the white man's bullets. Sometimes the charm would be in a war bonnet or a breech clout or perhaps a smooth pebble from the river. But charms could not be bought. Captain Aubry traded six red beads and a tin cup to one Indian brave for a war bonnet of eagle feathers. There was, perhaps, no charm in that particular bonnet, but it was a big one. As the Captain stood holding it in his hands the eagle feathers trailed on the ground.

Soon we were on the Cimarron Cut-off and were building our cooking fires with buffalo chips.[4] My chore was to gather the buffalo chips.[5] I would stand back and kick them, then reach down and gather them carefully, for under them lived big spiders and centipedes. Sometimes scorpions ran from beneath them. I would fill my long full dress skirt with the evening's fuel and take it back to mother.

It was on this trip that I made my first acquaintance with the big hairy spider called a tarantula. They lived in holes in the ground. When we found such a hole we would stamp on the ground close beside it and say, "Tarantula, tarantula! Come out! Come out. Tell us what it is all about." And sure enough they would come out walking on long stilt-like legs. As a reward for having obeyed we would kill them.

Sometimes little jeweled lizards would dart across our path, to stop, panting, in the shade of a scanty bush. Birds with long tails would walk the trail before us; walk upright and faster then our mules could walk. The drivers called them road-runners.[6]

We left the beautiful grassland behind us and struck in a south-westerly direction for the Arkansas River.

25

There was less and less forage for our mules and horses. We found rattle snakes and a variety of cactus that resembled trees. Behind us were the wild asters, scarlet honeysuckle, and night blooming poppies. Here the saffron sand drifted endlessly. Sometimes a cactus, an old bone or a bunch of red grass caused the desert mirage to assume gigantic proportions.

Captain Aubry told us how the muddy water in the buffalo wallows had often saved human lives. "One dying of thirst," he said, "does not stop for gnats or impurities." Once we traveled two whole days without water and, thirsty child that I was, I felt sorrier for the straining mules than for myself. We were careful even with the water for coffee. Captain Aubry had taught us how to put two little sticks over the top of the coffee pot to keep it from boiling over. Mother, Will and I had to wash our face and hands in the same basin of water. Will washed last, for mother said he was dirtier.

After we had traveled for what seemed like an eternity across the hot, dry land, we awoke one morning to find the air filled with a cool, misty rain. Although the cool, drizzling rain fell all day long it was a happy band that followed the Cimarron Cut-off. In the late afternoon we found our wagons winding in and out among some dwarfed cedar trees that grew on a flat mesa. There were a dozen Indian lodges there, and we saw the smoke issuing from the top of the lodges. We saw Indian children slither through the wet drizzle, among the stunted trees and the lodges. Someway it seemed we had entered a strange land of enchantment. This was different from anything we had seen. Often in looking backward I wonder what the feeling was that possessed me.

That evening when Captain Aubry came to sit at our fireside, he told us we were now in New Mexico Territory. "This is the land," said Captain Aubry, "where only the brave or the criminal come. This is called, 'the Land without Law.' But it is a land that has brought healing to the hearts of many. Many an invalid I have had in my caravans, but before they reached Santa Fé they were

26

eating buffalo meat raw and sleeping soundly under their blankets. There is something in the air of New Mexico that makes the blood red, the heart to beat high and the eyes to look upward. Folks don't come here to die—they come to live and they get what they come for."

The two weeks delay at Pawnee Rock made us late getting to Fort Union.[7] Biting winds gnawed at the open prairies, and frenzied snow had begun to surge up the dry arroyos before we came to where Fort Union lay patterned in black against a snowy background. How glad we were to see its tall stockade before us. It looked like a great black city within a high stockade. Yet Fort Union had been established only the year before, in 1851. It was thirty miles north of Las Vegas, and was built to be the headquarters for the Ninth Military Department. The establishment of Fort Union was the first effective measure taken against the Indians of that region. The war between the Americans and the murderous Apache had flamed blood-red, and Uncle Sam was trying hard to protect his traveling public.

That fort became the base for United States troops during the long period required to Americanize the territory of New Mexico. My own life story and the story of Fort Union have been strangely interwoven.

Fort Union was built in the form of a square. The officers quarters were constructed of logs, adobe and stone. They were arranged on the east and west sides of the square. The barracks were of adobe and were at the rear of the officers' quarters. The store buildings and the stables were on the north side and they, too, were of adobe. Outside of the square to the east, and entirely separate therefrom, was the hospital. About three quarters of a miles to the northwest were four buildings constituting the great arsenal, in which were kept for so many years the military stores for the whole southwestern army.

In the center of the parade ground stood a band stand, and on the north and the south of the parade ground were two wells from which the water supply of the garrison was secured. This supply was sometimes augmented by

27

hauling water from a spring about half a mile west. During the Civil War breastworks of earth were thrown up around Fort Union, and a tunnel was dug that connected it with the spring. Entrance to the Fort was on the south side.

The Cimarron Trail over which we came skirted the fort on the west side. On this side were the buildings of the traders, freighters and other civilians. John Dent, brother of the famous Julia Dent, wife of General U. S. Grant, was post trader at Fort Union for many years. All the trails from the Missouri River bearing southwest converged at Fort Union. It was headquarters and general supply depot for all the western region.

At Fort Union our great cavalcade rested. The tired mules were turned out to graze on the prairies. Freight was unloaded and the two hundred horses turned into the corral. Army officers came out and perched on the fence to look over and choose their horses. The parade ground was a shambles of bales of buffalo hides, Mexican blankets and sheep pelts, things to be sent out on the outgoing east bound train that was camped there. Our unloaded freight was piled separately and soldiers were busy unpacking and arranging.

Our camp was outside the gate that stood open and all day Will and I came and went as we pleased. Two friendly Indians sat and played mumblety-peg on a spread blanket. Will joined them and lost all his marbles.

One night while we camped at Fort Union the Indians attacked the stage station located two miles from the fort. We were awakened by the noise of departing troops. Mother helped us dress and we stood shivering with cold and fright inside the stockade and saw the flames of the burning stage station mount higher and higher. We heard the war whoops of the Indians and the shots of the soldiers. The troops did not return to the fort until the next day. They reported that one of the stock-tenders had been scalped and all the horses stolen. The stables were burned to the ground.

After a time when the mules were rested, we struck the westward trail again for there were supplies to be delivered at Santa Fé and gold to be dug at Sutter's Fort in California. We left Fort Union on a cold December morning. Sitting well-bundled on the seat beside mother I saw the long white trail of our wagons wiggling along ahead of and behind us. The frozen ground rang beneath the wheels of our wagons. The sounds of children's voices were like Alpine bells ringing.

I am glad today that I did not know that December morning what lay before us. We who walk life's highway are really very stupid. We know so much about philosophy and politics, but of whence we came and whither we go, we know nothing. Perhaps it is better, for God in His infinite kindness keeps the rainbow to guide us.

How our hearts waited for a sight of the Santa Fé of our dreams. We thought it would be a city, and waited breathlessly for the first sight of towers and tall turrets. We were in Santa Fé before we knew it. We crossed a water ditch where half-naked children stood unashamed and unfrozen to watch us. Then we passed through a great wooden gateway that arched high above us. We moved along narrow alley-like streets past iron-barred windows. We were among a scattering of low, square-cornered adobe houses. We saw a church with two cupolas. Mexicans, Indians, and half-breeds shouldered by us. We saw strings of red peppers drying, and brown babies asleep by old adobe walls.

Our caravan wriggled through donkeys, goats and Mexican chickens. We came to the plaza and found there a man, a tall man, leaning on a long rifle. He had a neck like a turkey, red and wrinkled, but he was the boss of the plaza. We went where he told us. Under his guidance, wagon after wagon fell into place. Dogs barked at us. Big-eyed children stared at us. Black-shawled women smiled shyly at us. We were in Santa Fé. Because bedlam seemed let loose, mother did not let Will and me out of the wagon until the mules were unhitched and led from the plaza.

As evening progressed young señoritas in crimson skirts, their black, mane-like hair caught up with great combs began drifting languorously by. Tall vaqueros in sashes and peaked hats strolled among the wagons. Mother resented the vaqueros. She tried to shoo them away like chickens, for she did not speak Spanish.

As darkness deepened Santa Fé threw off her lassitude. Lights glowed in saloons and pool-halls and in the Fonda, a great mud-walled inn. As soon as our freight was delivered at the customs house, our drivers began eagerly to sign up and draw their wages. They washed their faces and combed their hair. Pierre even drew the comb through his choppy mustache. There was a great hunting for clean shirts and handkerchiefs. From a dance hall came the tinkle of guitar and mandolin, a *baile* was forming. The cold air smelled of dust and sweating mules. We slept in the wagon, or tried to, but the noise and confusion kept us awake; we missed Pierre, missed the comfort of his presence.

The first thing we saw the next morning was the twin cupolas of the church. They seemed like beckoning fingers, fingers that pointed away from the dust and the squalor to the high blue heaven.

Captain Aubry was killed in Santa Fé two years later on the evening of a day when he had returned from a trip to California. He was stabbed to death by Colonel Richard Weightman, as a result of a quarrel over a criticism Weightman had printed in his newspaper about Captain Aubry's explorations. Weightman was a distinguished soldier and a West Pointer, yet the thing that he did was unpardonable.[8]

Many tales are told of Captain Aubry's courage and prowess. They tell of his famous ride from the central plaza in Santa Fé to the court-house steps in Independence, Missouri. The ride was made on a bet that Captain Aubry could not make it in six days. He did make it, but he fell from his horse in sheer exhaustion. My heart swells with pride when I think of Captain Aubry. He was my friend. He led mighty caravans across the prairies and in his heart was the lure of dim trails.

CHAPTER THREE

Life in Santa Fe 1852-1856

WITH THE vision of Sutter's Fort to lure us we continued on our long trek. One evening as we drew near to Albuquerque, the train went into camp at a large ranch house by the trail. Just across the road from us a detachment of soldiers under Colonel E. V. Sumner was camped, their white tents in precise rows.9 That evening a Mexican boy who was employed at the ranch visited our train. He stayed around our little tent talking and playing with Will until bedtime.

After he had gone mother discovered that a small workbasket in which she kept her money and jewels was gone. She carried her grievance to the wagon master who suspected the Mexican boy at once. The lad, upon being accused, admitted the theft, but said that one of Colonel Sumner's soldiers had taken the basket and its contents away from him. Colonel Sumner was then appealed to. He summoned the guilty soldier to his tent and held him there while search was made. The basket and part of the jewelry was found. The jewelry had no great value as it was mostly old yellow gold, family heirlooms.

Many years later a gold necklace set with amethysts was found in a shop window in Santa Fé. It had belonged to my Aunt Mary Rice. No part of the money was ever discovered. I was too young to realize what the loss of the money meant to my mother, but I do remember the shadow that settled on her bright face as we journeyed on to Albuquerque. She was alone in a strange wild land with two little children, and little children were not much of an asset.

During that ride to Albuquerque she was silent making her great decision. When we reached Albuquerque she left the train that was to have carried her to the gold fields of California. Will and I went with her house hunting. I remember the tears that rolled down her white set face when she sold a great yellow brooch and a pair of earrings that were heirlooms. She rented an old adobe house on the outskirts of Albuquerque and began taking in boarders. Most of her boarders were Indian scouts.[10]

Albuquerque was old even in 1852. It had been founded by the Spanish in 1706 and was named in honor of the Duke of Albuquerque. Don Francisco Fernandez, Duke of Albuquerque, was the 34th Viceroy of New Spain.

The houses in Albuquerque were like those in Santa Fé, the typical mud houses the Mexican builds everywhere. The one mother rented had six large rooms all in a row facing east. I remember the morning Pierre carried our luggage into the mud house and left it in a pile on the dust floor. He stood looking at mother for a moment. He tried to say something but his choppy mustache only wiggled. He kept turning his black hat round and round as he stood there. Mother tried to say something. She tried to tell him how kind he had been to us, but as usual when mother was stirred deeply, she was silent, pressing her hand to her throat as if choking. Will and I stood in the bare windswept yard watching the long wagon train pull westward. When we turned back our surroundings seemed desolate. Even today there are times when in my sleep that heart-breaking desolation falls on me. I am again in Albuquerque watching a wagon train pull westward without me. How glad I am to waken.

Mother set her brave hands to the plow and there was no looking backward. We went to work with a will, and soon were busy cleaning and whitewashing our little adobe, not knowing then how many mud palaces were to

32

be ours in the future, or that in time we would come to love them: Love their comfortable warmth in the winter, their coolness in the summer. The whitewashed walls were thick and uneven. The window embrasures were deep and we filled them with the Mexicans' red geraniums. In the beginning mother was able to get only five Indian scouts to board. They paid her $40.00 per month board, and sometimes they would be gone for weeks on scouting expeditions. They were all white men who knew well the ways of the red men. In the beginning mother did not board Mexicans, however as the months drifted by and she came to know them she felt differently. At first the darkness of their skin and the strange tongue they spoke confused her.

Our boarding house was kept very clean. Mother always said that cleanliness was next to Godliness. The dining table she placed in the center of the long living room. It was a long home-made wooden table covered with a yellow patterned oil cloth. At each plate she placed a heavy crockery plate, steel knives and forks with bone handles. The salt and pepper shakers were of tin with little handles. The cups of crockery were heavy and large. The food was served in deep dishes. Our boarders were polite and deferential, if sometimes clumsy and awkward. They treated little mother with respect and consideration. I remember how they tucked their hats under their arms when they came through the low doorway.

Mother was not long in learning the strange New Mexican cookery. In addition to the ever-present potatoes, gravy and dried apple pie, she served goat meat and mutton, Indian beans or frijoles. She learned to make tortillas, and cook dried choke cherries which seemed to be all seed and no berry. One dish our boarders craved was boiled wheat mixed with red pepper pods and cubes of goat meat. For breakfast we often had *atole*, a mush made from blue Indian corn.

One day in that memorable summer of 1853, mother sent me to the little store on an errand. It was necessary to pass the door of the Overland Stage Station and I saw a young white woman sitting on a bench by the door with a baby on her lap. I never could pass a baby by, so I sidled along the benches and offered my fingers for the baby's inspection. The baby was friendly and grasped my fingers warmly but the woman did not seem to see me. She seemed wrapt in some inward horror. She was a young woman and she had red hair like the baby. Although she had on a faded calico dress and her slender shoulders were stooped and discouraged looking, I think she would have been beautiful if it were not for the horror that lay in her eyes. She was like some beautiful bright thing maimed and broken. I loosed the baby's finger and slipped away for suddenly I wanted to cry. Once I looked back over my shoulder, but her inward horror remained undisturbed. I do not believe that she had once seen me or that she knew that she held in her lap a red-headed baby.

That evening one of the soldier-scouts told us about her. He said she was a Mrs. Adelaide Wilson. That she had been born in Alton, Illinois. In the year 1837 she had come with her father and mother to Texas where she spent her girlhood. She lost both her parents in an Indian massacre in Texas, and then had been forced to work for her board until she was sixteen. Then she met and married a young Texan by the name of Wilson. Happiness had come to the little red-haired girl at last.

Two years after her marriage, twin sons were born to the Wilsons. When the twins were two years of age, the little family joined an emigrant train enroute to California. After the train reached the plains of the Indian territory, young Mr. Wilson quarrelled with the wagon master and decided to turn back to Texas. The wagon-master tried to warn him. He told him it was dangerous and there was only safety in numbers, but Mr. Wilson would not listen. He turned back and the lone wagon was attacked by the Indians. Twenty-two year old Mrs. Wilson who had lost both her parents through the cruelty of the red man, now saw her young husband and her little twin boys scalped and murdered. She was taken prisoner.

34

She heard the Indians quarreling among themselves as to whose belt should be adorned with her long red hair. All day they drove her ahead of them like a sheep to the slaughter. All day as she stumbled she thought of her husband's body flung face up across the wagon tongue. She saw the little boys flung murdered beside him. When she turned she saw their scalps at the belt of her torturers.

That night in camp, while the Indians slept, she managed to sever her long braids from her head, and by so doing she saved her life. The Indians were disgusted, and one of them slapped her, but they took the long braids she had severed. By the evening of the second day she knew she would die if help did not come to her soon. As darkness came on she stumbled ahead of her captors down the bank of a little stream. Scrub cedar and wild plum trees grew there, and directly in her path stood an old hollow log. Much as a wounded animal creeps dumbly off to die alone Mrs. Wilson crept into the log. She supposed they would find and kill her, but that did not matter. She fell asleep at once. Perhaps the Indians did hunt for her, perhaps they did not really care if she escaped them. Mrs. Wilson never knew, for she lay and slept while red wood ants stung her, and the close quarters cramped her.

In the morning she heard the howling of the prairie coyote. She crawled from her hiding place to find the Indians gone. She ate the wild red plums and drank the clear creek water. She thought of returning to the wrecked wagon, but life is strong within us when we are but twenty, and she sought instead and followed the Albuquerque trail. Her unborn child stirred within her and she feared another night alone on the prairie. Yet another night came on and found her spent and weary. She sought shelter under the overhanging bank of the little stream. What thoughts were hers as she crouched there we can only guess. She heard the padded footfalls of the coyotes and the beating of her own heart as she listened.

Next morning a party of Mexicans enroute to the Navaho Reservation overtook her. They were kind and found her a place in their wagon, but her new little baby was born before they reached Albuquerque. I listened spellbound to the story the Indian scout told about her. I thought of the sad eyes of the young mother and of the little twin boys who had been left unburied out there on the wide prairie. I registered my first black mark against the red man.

Will and I soon fitted into the life at Albuquerque. We played with the Mexican children. We built make-believe forts with them and shot many an arrow at imaginary Indians. The trail over which we had come held a fascination for us. We played along it as far as mother would let us. Sometimes we would find a dry land terrapin. They loved to walk slowly along the trail that led westward. We wondered if they had come all the way from Fort Leavenworth. When we touched them they drew their heads back in their shells. We sometimes stood barefooted upon them.

Our adobe house stood with its back to the street, or road I suppose you would call it. Neither door nor window graced that long side. A Mexican loves privacy. One night when the scouts were all gone on reconnoitering expeditions and we were alone, Mother became frightened. She awoke in the night to hear an oft-repeated and unusual noise. It sounded like a pack rat working. Mother arose and lighted a candle. The noise stopped in a moment. She looked around and seeing nothing amiss went back to bed again, only to have the queer noise start over again. This time she arose in the darkness and walking softly discovered the noise came from where a big trunk was sitting against that windowless wall. Again she lighted a candle. She pulled the trunk forward and discovered a yawning black hole staring at her. Some one outside had been digging through the adobe wall seeking entrance. The hole was not large enough to permit a man's body. It was lucky mother had awakened. She was frightened but courageous. She nailed the front door and hung her silver teaspoons tied together to the latch string. They were to be the alarm if the marauders sought entrance at the door. She loaded a rifle and sat with it on her lap by the hole in the wall until morning. Next morning we found in the great heap of soft earth they had dug and piled outside by the opening some footprints. They were not the footprints of Indians. We found tracks of a man, a large man with shoes, a barefooted man and a burro. Who were they? Why were they burrowing through the walls of a little adobe house? Mother had no money, nothing of value. We never found out who the intruders were, but mother was always fearful when our boarders were all gone at once.

The life we lived in Albuquerque was not much like life in New Mexico now. The early-day Mexican did not much resemble the present day Spanish-American in whose veins flows so much Anglo-Saxon blood. The old Mexican was pure Spanish and Indian, and often the Indian blood predominated; a class of people as colorful as the land in which they lived.

This was a land of vast spaces and long silences, a dessert land of red bluffs and brilliant flowering cactus. The hot sun poured down. This land belonged to the very old Gods. They came on summer evenings, unseen, to rest their eyes and their hearts on the milky opal and smoky blue of the desert. For this was a land of enchantment, where Gods walked in the cool of the evening. What did the Gods think of the wagon trains that came creeping like serpents, of the red men who watched with bitter eyes that vast immigration?

Most of those early day Mexicans were clean, much cleaner than the Indians. Their houses of mud—mud roof, mud walls and mud floors—were someway clean. The hard trampled floor was sprinkled with water and often covered with hand woven grass matting. Their Navajo rugs were used only as bed coverings. The Mexican women plastered the inner walls of the house with a kind of homemade whitewash called "jaspe." It was very white and lovely, but it came off readily when touched. For this reason they loved to tack a few yards of bright-colored cretonne around the lower part of the wall. It

37

had the effect of wainscoting. They colored the white jaspe with the red mud of the canyons, making a thick, red plaster. This they applied to the outer walls of their houses. It was a soft, terra-cotta red that today the Taos artists use in their pictures.

The Mexicans were Catholic almost without exception. It was the sainted Catholic Fathers who brought civilization to New Mexico. In a carefully arranged niche in their snowy walls would be found a small statue of the Christ-Child and the blessed Madonna. Before this little altar a candle would often be burning.

A single bed in a corner would be heaped high with Navajo hand woven blankets. As bed time came each member of the family would be given a blanket. He or she, would roll up in the blanket, Indian fashion, and curl up on the earthen floor. Always the bed with its corn husk mattress and remaining blanket was left for Papa and Mamma. The Mexican usually kept a small flock of sheep and a few goats from whose fleeces they wove blankets. Lovely blankets are made from the long, silky fibers of the Angora goat.

Their diet of goat meat and mutton was supplemented with venison and the flesh of the antelope. They cooked pinto beans with red pepper. They made flat little tortillas in the ashes of their hearths. Stoves were a luxury. They made huge loaves of golden brown bread which they baked in outside ovens that resembled bee hives. They had gardens where they raised beans, peppers, blue corn—called atole—and many kinds of pumpkins and squash which they dried for the winter. They gathered the wild plum and choke cherry and dried them.

They loved bright colors. Red geraniums bloomed in their windows. The men wore brightly colored shirts and wide leather belts; but the women wrapped themselves from head to foot in somber black. They wore Spanish shawls, deep-fringed and lovely. Sometimes today it seems to me as I watch the gaily dressed girls and the black clad men about me, that the sexes have changed places.

38

Outside each little mud hut was a little mud oven. Mexican women are the best bread bakers I have ever known. Outside each door red peppers hung drying. When not in use the beehive oven served a double purpose. It was used by the dogs for sleeping quarters. On hot summer days the brown babies and dogs shared the meager shade afforded by the low, little house. Mexicans loved children and were very, very kind to them. They were pleased at any attention or kindness shown their children and maintained discipline with kindness.

I think that after mother's rather frightening experience in Albuquerque she was always a wee bit afraid. When one of her boarders suggested that she move to Santa Fé where he was soon to be stationed, she gladly consented. In the spring of 1854, we moved to Santa Fé and mother leased a large adobe house on the central Plaza. That adobe house, our first home in Santa Fé was torn down later and the present New Mexico Art Museum erected in its place. We soon had our house filled with military boarders. They paid at the princely rate of $45.00 per month.[11]

The house that today is pointed out as the oldest house in Santa Fé was occupied in that year of 1854 by the family of an educated Spaniard whose name was Dometrico Pérez. Pérez was the son of a former territorial governor of New Mexico, Colonel Albino Pérez who preceded Governor Armijo. Armijo was killed and beheaded by the Pueblo Indians in 1837.[12]

In the northern part of Santa Fé were two large stone structures, then unfinished. They were to have been governmental headquarters, but for more than thirty years Congress failed to make the necessary appropriation. I do not know if they were ever finished.

The church of San Miguel, the oldest church in America was even then in 1854 decaying with age. Its cracked and tottering walls were supported by lovely hand-carved beams. The historical old church had been built some two hundred and fifty years before our arrival. Once it had been partially destroyed by a religious uprising. In

39

1880 an attempt was made to restore it; but in 1854 it was condemned and dangerous. Children were never permitted inside its tottering walls. Catholic services were held in the Cathedral of San Francisco. However, the priests always went to San Miguel for Mass. They went serenely knowing that God's love was about them. I remember how once a priest died and his funeral service was held in the old church of San Miguel. Only the priests and the nuns attended.

The old San Francisco cathedral was built in|the shape of a cross. The present cathedral was built around the walls of the old ones. After the new walls were in place, the old walls were carefully removed. The right wings of that cross belonged to the nuns and to the girl students. The left wings to Father Lamy and his swarm of brown boys.[13] Between the two wings was the high, narrow altar, mystic in its loveliness. In the back, over the arched entrance was a graceful stairway, hand-carved and beautiful. The making of that stairway is a legend the nuns love to tell. The legend says:

Years ago when the cathedral was erected, the space for the stairway was so limited that the carpenters refused to try to place a stairway there. But a stairway of some kind had to be erected so the sisters made a *novena*. This was a series of prayers, asking that God would see their great need and in His great wisdom give them a stairway. The faith of a nun is a thing of great wonder. They lay all their problems at the feet of the Blessed Redeemer. They rest secure in a faith that is whole, without blemish.

One day an old beggar appeared at the cathedral asking food. He seemed tired and weary. After the sisters had fed him, he told them how he was a carpenter out of work, and glad he would be to do any little job with a saw and a hammer that needed doing. Of course they thought at once of the stairway; they showed him the cramped narrow space and asked the old man if he could put any kind of a stairway there for them. The old man stood for a moment in silence then he nodded his white

40

head, reached out a gnarled hand and started to measure, his lips moving dumbly. They gave him an order on a Santa Fé lumber yard and told him to get the material he needed. Again he nodded silently, his gnarled hands still measuring.

Three days later a stairway had taken shape beneath his skilled fingers, a thing of marvelous grace and beauty. The sisters were delighted. They sought the old man to reward him. They never did find him. No lumber yard in Santa Fé had supplied lumber for the miraculous stairway. Examination by experts showed that no nails, screws or metal had been used in its construction. Rare and costly wood had been used in its construction, wood never found in early day New Mexico.[14]

That night in the chapel the old man stood before them, the light from a stained glass window falling upon him. He appeared for a moment but did not speak to them. They knew then, their novena had been answered. The old beggar was St. Joseph, he who practiced his carpenter trade along the shores of the Sea of Gallilee long, long ago.

Of course you may not believe me but the stairway stands today in all its fragile beauty, showing no signs of the footsteps that have used it.

A few years ago a little book, beautifully and wonderfully written fell into my hands. It was entitled, "Death Comes for the Archbishop," written by Willa Cather. Miss Cather referred to her Archbishop as Father Jean La Tour. We in Santa Fé knew him as Bishop Lamy. Bishop Lamy reached Santa Fé in the autumn of 1851 and was elevated to the archbishopric in 1875. Miss Cather's Father Vallient we knew as Father Vicario. I remember Father Vicario's grief when he was sent to Denver to become first bishop there. I remember how we all grieved at his departure.

Father Lamy was very saintly and good. We often saw his earnest young face bent over a book in his study window. We often heard him speaking earnestly to some dark-skinned convert. The Mexicans all over the terri-

41

tory seemed to worship Father Lamy. His spirituality and devout faith controlled that mass of seething humanity that could, perhaps, have been controlled in no other way. At dawn when the bell rang for early mass we would see him come to stand on the steps of the Cathedral. From crooked alleys and narrow streets his people came. Shambling furtive-eyed men and black-shawled women came, and he raised his hands and blessed them. His love-inspired prayers laid hold of their simple hearts and held them at the altar of his church. The lovely church altar meant much to the Mexicans and converted Indians—worship and adoration and mystery.

The human heart has ever felt, but never been able to understand the mystery of salvation. Father Lamy knew that, and he labored to keep alive the mystery and beauty of God's love in little Santa Fé. One cannot write of early day New Mexico without writing reverently of the Catholic Church—not if one would be just. Yet for my own part I have never been able to unite with any church. The myth of a godhead persists among iconoclasts. And the primitive impulse to believe in creation by the will of a Father clings to us. After all, what does it matter what we believe so long as we live charitably by the Golden Rule, help to feed the hungry and clothe the naked?

It was in the year 1852 that Bishop Lamy induced six Loretta nuns to leave the mother convent in Kentucky and to establish a school for girls in illiterate Santa Fé. They story of their pilgrimage is a story of heartache and pain. One died of cholera and was buried in Independence. Another became sick and had to return.

The school that the sisters established enrolled one hundred girls that first year; ninety-five little Mexican girls and five American ones. The five American girls were Barbara Price, Lizzie Enders, Captain Lewis's two daughters and myself. Of this enrollment ninety-nine were Catholic. The sisters called me rebukingly, albeit lovingly, "their little heretic." Many were the stories they told me of the ninety and nine who safely lay in the shelter of the fold.

Mother Magdalena was the first Mother Superior in Santa Fé and she was, I verily believe, the most loved sister I have ever known. We all adored her and vied with one another for her favor. Sister Johanna was my personal teacher, and I enjoyed her tender guidance. Later she was sent to Denver to help establish St. Mary's Academy.

During my second year at the Academy, Father Lamy's niece came out from the East and entered the cloister in Santa Fé. Many of the sisters were dignified and reserved, permitting no familiarity, but Sister Loisa as we called her was always gentle and kind. She seemed to love the sound of our chattering voices and we crowded like kittens around her. She used to permit me to slip my hands up under her veil to caress her soft clipped hair. I loved her.

Our uniforms at the Academy were rather varied. For every day we wore dark purplish ones, rather long and gathered tightly to a high-waisted belt. On feast days we had better grade black ones, and on holidays we blossomed out in rosy pink. All were made alike, simply, ankle length, rather full and high waisted. Even today I can see us, one hundred strong, in long, high-waisted dresses.

I have never forgotten how the sisters tried to instill into our hearts a little bit of culture, and the hard time they had so doing. They planned our lessons so that we might learn poise and self reliance along with readin', writin' and 'rithmetic. Textbooks were sometimes laid aside and our lessons went on with marvelous ease and quietness. Each day we were supposed to do something for others, to help others. It was there that I learned how much easier it is to act than to think. Contemplation defied me. Unholy thoughts came pressing up, not to be denied at the hour of contemplation. Shape after shape, grotesque and ugly, forced themselves into my child's mind. If you think contemplation is easy, just try it.

I remember with a smile our autograph albums. Mine had a red velvet covering with gilt letters reading, "In Remembrance," beneath two snowy hands. The sister

explained to us that an autograph album was the place to write lofty sentiments. Turning through my little album today I find in Bishop Lamy's lovely writing:
 "Remember thy Creator
  In the days of thy youth."
On the next page in a childish scrawl and signed,"Lizzie Enders," is this: "Cows like pumpkins,
 Calves like squash.
 I like you,
 I do, by Gosh."
Here is another:"I thought, I thought,
 I thought in vain,
 And so at last
 I sign my name.
  Carlotta Pérez."
Father Lamy had a small farm situated about six miles from Santa Fé. When we missed him from chapel the sister would tell us that Father had gone to his farm that he might pray for us. They said that everything of consequence that is ever done in the world must first be thought out in solitude, and that every great person must have his forty days alone in the wilderness. I think today that is the only successful way. And I remember how we learned to expect showers of blessings from Father Lamy's retreat to his farm. I also remember how rested and refreshed he looked when he returned.

Just outside of Santa Fé was a mud church called Rosario Chapel. One Corpus Christi Day our entire student body marched out there. The sisters had trained us long and carefully for a pageant. We were all dressed to represent some Bible character. I was to be the Queen of Sheba. They placed on my head the solid gold crown taken from the altar statue of the Virgin Mary. It was a trifle too small but Mother Magdalena made it large by increasing the opening in the back. I was properly impressed and carried my head high as I stumbled along through the dust to Rosario Chapel; but the crown was of pure and solid gold, and gold is heavy. Before the

44

pageant was over my neck and my shoulders were throb-
bing with pain, and all the time the statue of the Blessed
Virgin was standing disconsolate and lonely.

The sister lined us up for march just outside the Cathedral where we were to wait for the church bell to
sound one clear note. That was to be the signal for Bishop
Lamy's army of boys to join us. While we were standing
there so primly in our masquerade get-up, along came an
old fruit peddler. He was a deaf and dumb man and did
not understand what the occasion was. He tried to shake
the hand of each of us—shake the hands of one hundred
little girls! Some one giggled. Laughter ran down the line.
Bishop Lamy came then and led the old man tenderly
away.

We were taught in the Academy to do fine bead and
needle work. The material for Bishop Lamy's robes was
brought all the way from Leavenworth by wagon train.
The sisters made the robes by hand. Always they saved
the little left-over fragments for use in the sewing classes.
Sometimes we made little pin cushions and needle books
out of them. I made in those classes a very handsome
needle book out of a fragment of Father's robe. I marvel
at the little even stitches my seven year old fingers did
make. I have given the little souvenir of school days to a
grand-daughter who wears today the black robes of a
Benedictine sister. It rests today, the little souvenir, in
a Catholic museum.

Sometimes, while we sewed or did our Indian bead
work the sisters would tell us stories. I think that the
stories they told us were the sweetest and best ever told
to little girls and boys. One story they told us was of the
little Lord Jesus and a scarlet cactus apple.

Behind the church of San Miguel was the boy's school
that Will attended. He, too, was a "little heretic." Many
a time was he sent home by Father Lamy in disgrace for
lack of reverence or respect to the Catholic creed. While
this school was across the river from the girl's Academy,
it was not so far away that the boys did not come at
recess and climb upon the adobe wall and call to the

45

little girls across the river. This was against the rules, but boys and girls have defied such rules all their lives. In those days Will, who loved girls, said that he hated Father Lamy's school and it was not until later years that the seed Father Lamy had planted in his wayward heart took root and bore fruit. It never did in mine. I shall die a "little heretic."

Fronting Santa Fé's Central Plaza on the north was the Governor's Palace, a one story adobe structure surrounding an inner court. The Governor's Palace looked as if it might have been transplanted from medieval ages. It had been the residence of territorial governors for years. One end strongly barred and bolted was used for a jail. One evening a political prisoner who was being held there called to me as I passed on my way home from school.[15] He sat just inside the barred doorway, an unlighted cigarette in his hand. Perhaps he was lonesome and wanted to talk to some one so badly that even a child would do. I lingered a moment as he tried to entertain me. He sang, I remember, "Shoo fly, don't bother I," and when I laughed at him he took out his great silver watch to show me. He told me he had a little girl at home waiting for him. He said that her braids were as long as mine but that hers were yellow, like gold. When he talked of his daughter his blue eyes looked troubled. His voice soft and gentle.

I went home to tell mother; perhaps she would give me a cookie to take back to my friend, the prisoner. She only said to wait until morning. It was too late then to take cookies, for during the night, someone came softly close to the bars and shot my prisoner through the heart! It must have happened not long after darkness had fallen, for he still sat in his chair by the door, the unlighted cigarette on the floor by the tips of his fingers. I was the one to find him when I came bearing gifts in the morning. His head was sunken on his chest. I could not see his face, but I saw the clotted blood on his shirt front. We were told that often happened to political prisoners. He was killed, they said, to prevent his betrayal of State

46

secrets. We never knew the reason, but I have thought often of the child with the yellow hair who waited for the return of her father. The old Governor's Palace at Santa Fé holds many age-old secrets.[16]

It was in this old adobe palace that Lew Wallace, while Governor of New Mexico, found time to write *Ben Hur*. Perhaps the thick old walls whispered to him of lovely ladies, daring deeds and the healings performed by the Great Galilean. The old Governor's Palace has been turned into an historical museum, and if you look you will find there many beautiful relics of the days that are gone with the wind, of the days when Santa Fé was "The Fairest City on the Trail."

Will and I learned to play a fascinating game with the little Mexican and Indian children on the dusty streets. We played it with little sticks and pinto beans. It was called "kanute," and was a sort of crude variation of the American shell game. We both became adepts and I have never since seen a faker practicing the shell game that I have not wanted to try and beat him at his own game. I won the Indian children's red beads and then would have to sit on them to keep them from stealing them from me. I took the little Mexican children's trinkets and piñon nuts. If they cried too hard, I would give them back.

Kanute was a simple illustration of the old saying, "The motion of the hand is quicker than the eye." My hands flew like lightning among the sticks and beans. One day mother came upon me sitting upon a string of shell beads while in my lap was a heap of piñons; but I was too busy to see her coming. My sole adventure in gambling came to an abrupt halt.

Very near Santa Fé was old Fort Marcy,[17] built by the army under Colonel Price many years before. It had been used as a burial ground many years before during the Mexican War. Mexico had been subject to one revolution after another during the twenty-five years of her independence. Santa Fé, remote from the seat of government and ecclesiastical authority, had suffered many evils, the invariable result of such a situation. Fort

47

Marcy had been in ruins many years, but an old two-story building still stood there. Inside the building was another smaller one that was supposed to have been used by sharp shooters during the Mexican War. Erosion was opening many old graves in Fort Marcy. Some bleached old bones were lying there. With the savagery of children we gathered up the old bones and played a game we called, "Steal the Dead Man's Bones." When our parents found it out the bones were taken from us. 'Tis a fantastic thing to remember. I remember once in Fort Marcy falling into the old cistern. That is all I remember, of how I got out, or who helped me, I haven't the haziest recollection.

One dear old lady in Santa Fé, a Mrs. Sutton, had a nineteen year old son buried in Fort Marcy. He had been a drummer boy in the Civil War. After serving through the war he had come home, and had been bitten by a mad dog on the streets of Santa Fé. He died of hydrophobia.

The loss of her only child unhinged Mrs. Sutton's mind. She became a town character both loved and laughed at. She was tall and stooped, sparse-haired. She wore a switch and had kindly confiding blue eyes. She went daily to Fort Marcy climbing the steep hill slowly, to place flowers or some little offering on her son's grave. She had erected a little shelter there of rocks and sometimes on dark nights she would go to place a lighted lantern there. She once told me confidentially that her son had always been afraid of the dark. Sometimes I accompanied her on her pilgrimages to the shrine of the grave. She seemed to like having me and always called me "sis." I called her San Tannie and we were great companions.

They said that Mrs. Sutton had been made the butt of a rather cruel joke. Shortly after her son's death, when her heart was torn with grief, an old Mexican woman knocked on her door. She held in her arms a dark infant. She told Mrs. Sutton that the babe was her dead son's child. Would she please raise it as the girl-mother was an unwed mother? Mr. Sutton scarcely believed it but after all, one never knows. If the dark babe was her grandchild she wanted it. She raised the baby as her own, lavishing upon it all the love of her heart. The passing years revealed that the old Mexican woman had not spoken truly. The babe was all old Mexico-Mexican, and as he grew into manhood was forever and ever getting into trouble. This meant grief for San Tannie; between grief and worry she became unbalanced.

She was a Methodist. The Catholic church was anathema to her. Her only consolation seemed to be in reading her Bible and singing old Methodist hymns. All that was needed to start her off on a long Methodist sermon was to say something nice about the Holy Catholic Church. The sisters smiled and listened to her sermons. They loved and took care of her.

As the years went by she became more and more senile. Finally the sisters had her baptised into the Catholic church. They took excellent care of her and she never seemed to know that she was a Catholic; that is until the night of her death. She had lain for hours without moving or speaking, when suddenly it seemed that the mists that had obscured her mind lifted. She sat up in bed, looked at the cross around her neck and the priest bending over her. She cast the crucific from her, thrust the priest aside, walked to the window and leaped to her death.

Over the years another memory returns: the candy counter in a store at Santa Fé. The candy was in glass show cases safe from small prying fingers. There was red candy, white candy and striped candy. There was candy heaped, piled and scattered all over. O, the glorious sight and smell of it! There were licorice sticks and licorice in jet black strings like shoe strings. There was licorice in the shape of fat negro babies. Lovely, delicious licorice that left stains on the fingers and behind the ears of the children. There were candy hearts with love verses written on them. There was horehound candy in long brown waxen sticks. There was peppermint candy and wintergreen candy. There were tiny dots of red candy so hot that when one ate it, it was was best to go and stand

49

with mouth wide open so the wind could blow in it. There was candy that looked like shelled corn. There was white chewing wax and sweet caporal and sen-sen.

On the walls of this magical store were calendar pictures that advertised the wonders of products behind the long counter. O, the dirty, dirty man who sat writing a letter! We looked right over his shoulder, "Dear Mr. Packer," he wrote, "Ten years ago I washed my face with Packer's tar soap. I have never used soap since."

There was the picture of a clean little baby beneath which was written:

When baby was sick we gave her Castoria
When she grew older she cried for Castoria
When she had children she gave them Castoria.

There was another picture of a fat man in a white apron. He had a huge butcher knife and was carving a pink ham. Beneath his picture was written:

This is the butcher of Spotless Town.
We spotted a spot on the butcher's gown.
It would not be 'meet' for justice sake,
To roast the poor butcher at the stake,
Therefore behind the bars he shall go,
The bars of what? . . . Sapolio.

Strange are the things I remember, well-loved things, unimportant ones. Long poems that I learned and recited. A sack that had once held Bull Durham tobacco and became in time my holy of holies. It held a moss agate that Will found at Fort Marcy, a pebble that glittered from the Cimarron river—we called it a nugget—and there were three horse hairs wrapped round a chicken feather, that was a charm to keep away evil. Those were my treasures.

There came a night when I wound my way homeward from the Academy that a man met me. He seemed to have come down from the Mexican Plaza. He smiled at me gently with kind eyes. He shifted his hat to the back of his head and tried to engage me in conversation. I exchanged a few, simple, shy words with him. Later I was to be prouder of my acquaintance with this man than with any other, for he was Colonel Kit Carson. I think that our conversation that evening was mostly monologue on his part, for as usual I was tongue-tied in the presence of a stranger. I remember that he said, with a glance at my books and my uniform, "Them nuns do a heap sight of good in this god-forsaken country." Thus began a friendship that was to last as long as we lived, a friendship that stood me in good stead in later years when I married a young soldier and went to live at Camp Nickols. Kit Carson was then my husband's superior officer.[18]

Colonel Carson had come to New Mexico in 1826 when he was a lad of seventeen. He often told us about the hunting party with which he came west, and of how he had fallen in love with this wild beautiful land and had never left it. When I met him in that year of 1853 he was United States Indian Agent to the Utes and Apaches. Later, when the Civil War broke out, he was brevetted Brigadier General.

There, too, was Colonel Carson's girl-wife. History tells us that he married Maria Josefa Jaramillo of Taos, New Mexico. History also tells us that he had two Indian women or wives. That one of the Indian girls he married was called Waa-nibe, or Singing Grass, a Northern Arapahoe and the mother of his daughter, Adaline; the other Indian wife was a Cheyenne Indian girl whose name was "Making-Out-Road." He married this girl at Bent's old fort about 1840. She divorced him, according to Indian custom, by throwing his personal effects from her lodge. This is what history tells.

All that I know was that he had a little Mexican wife we called Little Jo. She was a lovely Mexican girl with heavy braids of dark hair. Her demure little face was round and brown and her great dark eyes were usually cast down. Colonel Carson called her Little Jo, and I am sure that he loved her very much.[19]

It was rumored in Santa Fé that he had a wife in Missouri, but how could that be when he was only seventeen

51

when he left there? Still Colonel Carson loved women and he seemed to take his loves where he found them. Looking back across the years I do not wonder at his love for Little Jo. I remember how his eyes grew tender when he looked at her. What American woman could have so filled the heart of that lonely pioneer, for Colonel Carson was a lonely man. His was a great heart and very kind, yet he wore shyness before his face like a veil. Only with children and the child-like Mexicans was he able to lay that shyness aside. It was natural that he should marry among the people he loved and protected.

Carson, the man whose memory we revere, was awkward and uncouth. Often he was coatless and perhaps did not own a tie. He spoke in the western vernacular. The pictures that I have of him are a child's memory of a virile Indian scout and a girl who knew nothing of the loveliness of her brown body.

Perhaps the greatest lesson nature offers us is that in the last analysis nothing is any more remarkable than anything else. I think there never has been a man, no matter how big, who did not have human frailities. The lesson biography teaches us is that great men surpass others because they refuse to falter. In the end they win out. Colonel Carson was my friend of whom I am proud.

My remembrance of our home in Santa Fé that first year is of a house frugally furnished but very clean. The uneven adobe walls were whitewashed; the window embrasures were deep as divans. Folded Indian blankets covered the wooden settees that flanked the fireplace. The fireplace, Mexican made, was of adobe and rather small. The fires that burned there were of fragrant cedar and piñon. The candles on the mantle were home-made of sheep's tallow and very large. They stood in two tin saucers and the melted tallow ran down their sides and into the saucers. The candle light in the evenings flickered over the dark beams of the ceiling and over mother's great pottery jar, or "tanaja."

I remember how mother made a great companion of me. She did not treat me as if I were a child, but as if I

52

were grown up. How hard I tried to be grown up. We were together all the time. She would pretend that I was a great help with the dusting, sweeping and cleaning. Looking back I am sure I was only a bother, but to hear us two talking with each other, you would have imagined there was a whole houseful of people. Sometimes we worked in the garden, weeding beets and onions, or we hoed among the squash and pumpkins. We practiced speaking Spanish and laughed at the mistakes we were forever making.

In the meantime, Will was growing up and was so tall that his clothing piece by piece was discarded. It seems as I look back that his hands always dangled a mile out of his sleeves. He was quiet and studious, and without any effort was speaking the Spanish tongue as fluently as the Mexicans. I remember the evenings that we so much enjoyed. The days were hot, long and busy. In the evenings we lighted the candles. Through open door and windows drifted the music of the ever-present Mexican mandolin. In the evening mother read to us, or spoke of the home we left on the bank of the muddy Missouri. Sometimes in the evenings Will would go to the Plaza with other boys, but Mother kept me with her.

The narrow streets were hot and dusty. Discouraged flea-bitten curs and frousy chickens would dispute the right-of-way with flamboyant Mexican roosters. Goats and small burros lay unmolested on the narrow board walks.

Santa Fé was at that time the supply center for all the surrounding country. Originally a part of New Spain it showed the Spanish influence. Kaolin and coal mines were in the vicinity, and its trade extended to far-away California. Freight wagons pulled in daily from the Staked Plains of Texas, from Fort Union and California. Great caravans were leaving for the east, west and south. Friendly Indians came in for the trading. Often the narrow streets became choked with a wiggling mass of humanity. Sometimes in the night we would be awakened by some piercing scream or long-drawn wail, and would expect to hear the next morning of some deed of unusual violence. But it was only some minor misfortune; a drunken Mexican chased by an Indian, or a white woman badly frightened.

In those days homeopathic remedies were used almost exclusively. One did not send for a doctor unless death threatened. Poultices for Will's aching chest were made from ground mustard mixed with water and spread on red flannel. His earache was treated by a drop of sweet oil and the sedative smoke from a pipe.

The boil on my back mother brought to a head quickly by an application of soft soap and sugar. A whole clove was inserted in a tooth that started aching. Smelling salts were handy for folks who felt faint. Burns were covered quickly with dry baking soda. Neuralgia yielded to a pillow filled with hops and heated hot in the oven. Stomach ache mother treated by liberal potions of pennyroyal tea or hot ginger. Cough syrup she made from the bark of the wild choke cherry infused with honey. As prevenative against croup, colds and contagion she hung a small bag of asafetida around the necks of her children. Its odor defies description.

She was not long in learning to use the Mexican cure-all "O-pshaw" that grew along the New Mexico rivers. Shampoo jelly was made from the wild soap weed. Puff balls were kept to stop bleeding. Sore throats were treated by wrapping a stocking around the neck—the dirtier the sock the better. The sole of the stocking was spread out as as near the sore tonsils as possible, the long leg was wrapped round and round. The soreness was supposed to vanish. Sometimes it did.

Scraped buffalo horn placed in a drunkard's whisky would certainly cure him of the habit—if it didn't kill him. Ten-penny nails, about six to a bottle of strong vinegar, made a blood tonic. The vinegar dissolved the nails. Take a teaspoonful of the tonic each night before retiring, it would put iron in your blood—and a curl in your hair.

The dried lining of a chicken gizzard powdered and mixed with clean sand from the river would grind ulcers right off your stomach. A cold door key dropped down your back without warning would stop nose bleeding. Warts rubbed witha stolen dish towel would disappear like magic.

Mother had great confidence in the potent qualities of a certain vegetable compound. Most ladies in those days thought that a baby was enclosed in every third bottle. Some ladies skipped the third bottle. The compound was good for all the things that ever could ail you. Nausea, kidney pains, spots before the eyes, bad taste in the mouth, nervousness, fear of impending evil, fainting spells, unnatural craving for food, the blues, headaches and what-have-you.[20]

The old pioneers had small need of doctors, being hardy they managed to survive homeopathic remedies.

The old adobe houses were mostly beg-bug infested. All day long they would hide in cracks and in crevices to come forth at night to crawl on you, to sting, bite and blister. One lady bed-bug could lay enough eggs to hatch out a million. Twice a week mother would carry our hand-carved wooden beds out and pour boiling water from the tea kettle where she thought it would do the most good. She would dip a henfeather in kerosene and oil the places not touched by the water. It was not long until she had them eliminated but she never rested but kept up the fight against them.

The beds were draped with mosquito netting canopies for screens were unknown. There were no fly-swatters but a small branch from a cottonwood was used to shoo flies from the table.

So many things worthwhile I cannot remember. So many doors of memory are locked, so many little doors fly open at a single touch; a heap of broken toys.

The market place in Santa Fé was a wonder. In open air booths lay piles of food stuffs. Heaps of red and green peppers vied with heaps of red and blue corn and heaps of golden melons. There were colorful rugs woven by the hands of the Mexicans and deep-fringed shawls, gay with embroidery. There were massive Indian jars filled to the brim with Mexican beans. There were strings of prayer beads from old Mexico, beads worn smooth and shiny to a patina by many praying hands. Mexican turquoise in heavy settings of silver. Silver was then cheaper than tin. Here was to be found exquisite Mexican drawn work and intricate Indian bead work.

In deep, old hand-carved frames were pictures, mottoes, wreaths of flowers all cunningly fashioned of human hair, red, black, brown and yellow. There were beaded moccasins and chamois coats, leather trousers, silver trimmed saddles, spurs and knapsacks; great hand-carved chests and cupboards, Indian baskets and jars without number. So many things that were fine and splendid; so many things that were rude and clumsy, the Santa Fé market afforded.

If one were in quest of a pair of Indian moccasins he might hunt among booths until he was dizzy, only at last to come to a heap of footwear of every size, shape and quality and in such abundance as to make him forget what he came for.

Long lines of burros all but hidden under enormous bundles of fagots made headway in and out among the children, taking good care not to step on them.

This was old Santa Fé, asleep among the red hills. Sheep grazed on distant mesas, a hot wind blew across the mesquite. There were saw-tooth mountains silhouetted against the sky. Through a great wooden gateway flowed the Santa Fé trail from across a wide, hot valley.

From September of the year 1852, until August of 1856, we lived in New Mexico. Will and I had three years in the Catholic school. We learned to speak the Spanish language. Unconsciously we had learned to love the land of great distances and long silences. We had become familiar with the sunsets and great dawns that burn down into the valley and that flame up over the blue mountains. The stunted thorn trees, the sand that reflects sun

56

like polished metal, and the thin gray lines that writhe in the heat waves like a nest of spiders, we loved without knowing we loved.

When mother received a letter saying that her home in Missouri was standing unrented and was fast falling into decrepitude, she decided to return there and forget her dream of California. When she told Will and me what she was planning we didn't mind, for we thought only how nice it would be to hit the trail again. We did not realize how homesick we would be for New Mexico before we would come again to Santa Fé.

CHAPTER FOUR

Fort Leavenworth 1856-1860

On a hot August day in 1856 we left Santa Fé for Fort
Leavenworth. This time we took passage in a small train
of twenty wagons—too small for adequate protection
from the Indians. The wagons were all ox-drawn and
oxen do not walk as fast as mules or horses; however,
they did walk more evenly and we were able to sew or
even read as they ambled slowly eastward. The east-
bound wagons were not so heavily laden. We slept in our
covered wagon although many wagons held bales of buffalo hides for eastern markets.

On this trip across the Great Plains I was eleven years
of age and Will was thirteen. We read and reread *Pil-
grim's Progress* and a travel book written by some missionary. It told of natives spearing fish off coral ledges,
of hibiscus blossoms and snakes so large they might have
swallowed our covered wagon.

Will walked all day by the wagons. Mother busied
herself sewing ball after ball of rags to be woven when
reaching home into a fine rag carpet. I think that the
walking and carpet rag sewing helped them to kill the
time as the slow oxen bore us onward. I had nothing to
do but help with the carpet rag sewing, a task that I
loathed.

It is a most remarkable thing that today I can find
nothing outstanding about that trip eastward. Folks tell

me it must have been an unique adventure, and beg to hear about it. I assure you it was often tiresome and boring. August is the hot time of the year and I think I shall never forget how I sweated under the canvas curtain. I remember Mother's flushed face as she bent over her sewing, and how I wound the long rag rope into tight, hard balls for her. I can see Will trudging wearily close beside the wagon. I can see the hot August sun shining on the polished horns of the red and white oxen. Slowly we passed Fort Union and slid slowly down in a valley. How small and forlorn seemed our string of twenty white covered wagons.

When we reached Walnut Creek on the plains of western Kansas we found that a small store, surrounded by a cluster of cabins, had been built since our passing four years before. On a level table land behind the store some Apache Indians were camping. Some of them followed us from the store to our wagon begging for the groceries we had bought from the trader. When mother refused to part with the food she had bought the Indians became angry. When the wagon-master heard the loud voices he came to our assistance. A wicked-looking warrior hideously painted made a gesture as if he would lift the wagon master's scalp lock. The wagon master drew a knife and made a retaliating gesture of cutting the ugly warrior's throat from ear to ear. Muttering and sullen, the Indians moved back to the mesa. Although the wagon master laughed, he seemed a bit uneasy, especially when the trader came and reproved him for offending the Apaches.

Next morning there was no sign of the Indians on the mesa. They had disappeared in the night. We moved on with fear and reluctance. Mother, who knew what might be expected of Indians, put away her sewing and sat tense and alert in the wagon. Will was cautioned to walk close, within hand reach of the wagon. Mid-afternoon found the oxen suffering from the heat and the wagon master decided to make camp under the shade of some tall cottonwood trees, saying that after the hot sun had

60

gone they would journey onward, as there was to be a full August moon.

The women were delighted to use the time to do a bit of laundry. Soon bushes were full of blue shirts, gingham dresses and aprons. On the buffalo grass were spread the dish towels. The children were delighted to be free to roll and to tumble. The games that we played when the wagons spewed us forth night and morning!

When the day cooled and the fresh-washed clothing was brought from bush and brier, an early supper was prepared and eaten, beds were arranged for the women and children in the wagons. The full moon arose that night and looked down upon twenty covered wagons creeping along the Santa Fé Trail eastward, all passengers sound asleep. Only the men-folks plodding by the side of the oxen were awake. The out-riders nodded in their saddles.

In the wee, small hours we were awakened by the hideous war cry of the Apaches. At that frightful cry the stupid oxen swung from the trail, wooden yokes and long horns clashing. Our wagon bed rose and hung suspended in the air like Mohammed's coffin. Had we left the running gears behind us? No, with a bounce and a jolt we made connection. Our driver cursed and shouted. The Indians continued to utter their war whoops. The oxen stampeded blindly and ran themselves into exhaustion. Mother tried to get Will and me into her arms but we succeeded only in striking first one and then the other in the upheaving wagon. After a time the tired oxen quit running and the Indians quit screaming. Dawn came and found twenty wagons scattered in confusion over the prairies.

Patiently the out-riders brought us back to our place on the Santa Fé Trail. We continued our way eastward; but fear came and rode with us. Why the Indians had not massacred us when they had us at their mercy, we did not know. Were they afraid of the punishment that would surely be meted out to them? An Apache is not much afraid of anything. Had there only been a few of the Indians and had they been afraid to attack without

61

plenty of warriors? Had they gone to increase their numbers? Would they attack again at the first instance? We did not know, and our apprehension grew. Mother said that never again would she start across the prairies except in a big train. We remembered what Captain Aubry told us, and were sorry we had not heeded.

In a place on the Kansas prairies we came to a tall ramshackle house. Decrepit it seemed. At first we thought it abandoned for weeds grew to its very door and loose boards flopped from the windows. However, as we came nearer we saw several men lounging in its scanty shade. When our wagon-master asked if we might draw water from the well in the yard they seemed sullen and taciturn. They gave us permission to draw the water but did not seem to want to enter into conversation. We watered the oxen and went into camp across the trail from them.

As we ate our lunch and rested in the shade of the wagons a woman came furtively from the house. She was a faded, bedraggled creature. I shall always remember the hopeless look of longing in her eyes as she talked to us. She crept under our wagon and reached out a workworn hand and touched mother's hand timidly. In a half-pleading whisper she asked mother to stay with her until her expected baby was born. She would hesitate, as she pleaded, to cast fearful looks at the men lounging in the shade of the house. Mother was surprised and said, "No, I could not think of it. We are on our way to Kansas City." The woman's voice faltered when she answered saying, "I am in danger here. I cannot tell you about it. My husband would kill me." When one of the sinister fellows arose and came toward us the woman arose and went dejectedly to meet him.

Mother went at once to the wagon-master with the woman's strange story. He heard her in silence and then went to talk to the woman's husband. When he came back he said that he told the man he would make room in our caravan for his wife. It was only sensible that she should go to town or where she could have the care she so soon would be needing. The man's only answer was a

62

steady flow of curses. So it was that we touched briefly on some secret of the prairie.

As we neared fateful Pawnee Rock in mid-afternoon, Will, who was walking close to the wagon espied a small trapper's cabin set among bushes not far from the trail. We saw him turn out and walk to the half-opened door. Mother called to him for she was always afraid of an Indian ambush. But he approached the cabin and knocked at the half-opened door. Receiving no answer he attempted to enter. He staggered backward and called out, "Oh, mother!" Mother thought he had been struck by an arrow and she started climbing down from the wagon while the oxen still plodded onward. Some of the walking men joined Will quickly and found stark tragedy inside the little cabin. The bodies of two white trappers lay there. One body was just inside the door; another lay on the rude bunk in the corner. The massacre had taken place not long before our train's arrival for both bodies were warm and limber. Blood oozed from their freshly scalped heads. Evidently the approach of our caravan had frightened away the red devils. A fire still smoldered in a small, sheet-iron stove and a black pot of beans still simmered. The men had been trappers. Traps and guns hung from pegs in the wall. Someway the Indians had crept upon them as, unsuspectingly, they prepared their dinner.

Mother would not let me see the murdered men, although almost everyone else in the caravan went into the cabin. They all came out weeping. Such sights, mother said, were not for children. The wagon train camped by the cabin and burial was given to the poor trappers. The men made a great wide box with boards from the bunk, door and table. One deep, wide grave was dug. The women furnished clean white sheets to wrap the dead bodies. They were placed in the grave, one man's head at one end, the other at the other. The empty box was first lowered into the wide grave. Why this was done I do not remember, but I think because they did not have enough boards to make two boxes.

63

I remember a bit of the burial service. I remember we all sang while the white-sheeted bodies were lowered. I remember a man stood down in the grave balancing on the box edge and carefully arranged the bodies. I remember the clear voices that sounded to heaven, "Let me to Thy bosom fly," and, standing there by mother, I kept wondering if they had flown. I seemed to see God, great and awful standing with two sheeted forms in His arms. I wondered if, when Indians died, God would take them into His arms. It was a problem that I have never been able to solve to my entire satisfaction.

Next morning when our caravan moved onward I looked back through the rear opening of our covered wagon and wondered again about the "Dust to dust and ashes to ashes" I had heard in that first funeral sermon.

Now this year of 1856 was the first year of the John Brown disturbance and, as we wended our way slowly through the great state of Kansas, tales of the Border Ruffians reached us. Tales of their dreadful deeds, of murdered women and tortured children. As we reached more settled regions we found houses in ruins where smoke drifted from smoldering embers. The tales grew more frightening and evidence was on every hand that they were not tales that had been enlarged upon.

John Brown, it seems, was an abolitionist and crazy as a mad hatter. He seemed to have conceived the idea that he could free the slaves in a one-man campaign. Just then he was active in the border warfare carried on between Kansas and Missouri. Kansas seemed to hold the center of the map that summer.

An attempt was being made to turn the entire state into one massive vineyard. Experts said that the climate of Kansas was ideal for the culture of grapes and olives. Nebraska, it was claimed was too cold for either the olive or the vine. Utah, where it had been tried out, was branded as "too pre-occupied" and barren. New Mexico was only waste land, fit only for cactus. Big, level Kansas had a mild and genial climate, and it lay in the heart of the continent. Its fertile soil was capable of supporting

64

twenty million people. Freemen from the vineyards of Germany and Italy had been brought over and induced to take up the new industry. This mighty Kansas was to be made into the vineyard of the New World. No wonder the Ruffians fought over her.

There came at last an evening when our tired oxen stumbled to a halt at little Diamond Springs. Water bubbled from the earth as clear and sparkling as a diamond. It came in such quantity that a little stream had its source there. A great stone house stood near by, its windows boarded up, its massive door barred and bolted.

Our wagon-master went into a huddle with the drivers and it was decided that on account of the Border Ruffians and the danger from Indians that we should go into camp at Diamond Springs and stay there until such time as a larger caravan might join us or the Government be induced to send a detachment of soldiers to protect us. Some of the drivers argued against the delay. Many of them were anxious to get to Fort Leavenworth. However, we were guided by the decision of the wagon master.

Mother tried to say that she could not see where we could be in much more danger on the road than in camp; but being a woman no one listened to her. The man said that if we were to be attacked by Ruffians or Indians we would have the old stone house in which to seek shelter One argument led to another and finally it was decided to break the great lock and to enter.

We used that grand, old parlor as a community hall while we camped there. It had a fireplace at one end and a pathetic old spindle-legged piano at the other. Several ladies in our party played well and one old man had a fiddle. In the evening while flames leaped on the hearth, lilting tunes would go echoing through the empty rooms. The old man would take his fiddle out of its red-lined cradle. He would nestle it under his chin for a moment and then suddenly the Irish Washer Woman would begin ducking in and out among the smoke-blackened rafters. The old man teased the Washer Woman. The old rafters shook with the music. The fiddle would wail like a banshee, the old piano kept on a thrumming. The piano throbbed with love and with longing. The fiddle filled the hearts of the children with its strange mystery. Flames leapt on the hearth. Shadows danced on the stairs. Some folks danced their shoes a clump, clumping. This is my only memory of a strange fire-lit evening when the Santa Fé trail wound like a serpent through the New World's dream vineyards.

All of us were called upon to furnish entertainment. Two drivers agreed to furnish sheet music. They appeared at the piano-end of the long room with a bed sheet in their hands. They then lay down on the floor, covered themselves with the sheet and "snored". There were charades, jokes, dialogues, recitations and songs. Even Will and I were called upon for the songs and recitations we had learned at school in Santa Fé. It has been so long ago since we camped at Diamond Springs, and yet I think I can hear mother's clear voice singing the "Blue Bells of Scotland."

Near the old stone house was the crumbling ruins of a sod corral. A bit of Diamond Creek ran through it. Some of the oxen were usually standing there. In places the water had collected in small pools and had become stagnant. Tadpoles hatched out by the hundreds. The children loved to stand leaning against the sod walls and throw clods of earth at the tadpoles. One day as we stood there engaged in our favorite sport we saw two huge rattle snakes making a meal on tadpoles. We were delighted and began to throw clods at the snakes, thinking we were far away and behind a wall from them. It was great sport with enough thrill to make it dear to our hearts. As I stood pressed against the sod wall leaning far over to throw well, I heard a rattle that sounded much nearer than the snakes by the pool. Somewhere between my warm little stomach and the old wall was a furtive movement; again sounded that metallic buzzing. I drew back and there in a hole in the wall, was a huge rattler. Three inches from me was a flattened head with swollen jaws and a forked tongue striking at my blue dress. For a moment I was too terrified to move. For days I was ill from shock and fright. But never again have I played with rattle snakes.

In those days folks had some strange superstitions about rattle snakes. They said that if you pulled out the poison fangs of a rattler they would grow back in like the baby teeth of children. They said that if you were bitten by a rattler and didn't die, every year at the same season of the year you would break out in yellow and green spots like the spots on the skin of a rattler. They said that all day long you would go squirming and twisting like a serpent. If you had a tail no doubt you would rattle ... folks said.

There were many small snakes of the prairies, most of them harmless although we called them by many fear-inspiring names. There were blowing vipers, spreading adders, bull snakes, garter snakes and water snakes.

Once Will put his foot right down on a rattler. He was scared, but the snake did nothing. It did not even coil or strike out at him. This snake was certainly different. It lay still when Will removed his foot, lay still on the path to the milk house, and began slowly rattling its rattles. It fixed its great eyes on Will and flattened its head and stuck out its forked tongue and went on rattling its rattles. Suddenly from all around little snakes began to put in an appearance. There were a dozen or more of them. The old snake opened wide her jaws and the little ones disappeared down inside of her. When Will came to tell mother about what he had seen, she told him he had witnessed one of nature's miracles. "Great Jumpin' Grasshoppers," said Will with conviction.

After two weeks at Diamond Springs our food supply began running low, but still the men refused to press onward. Perhaps there is such a thing as mass panic for one evening when the advisability of breaking camp was discussed around the fireplace and a vote was taken most of the men voted to stay where we were. That was the evening mother arose to her small height and an-

67

nounced firmly that she was much more afraid of Old Man Famine than a host of Border Ruffians. She said she was very anxious to get back to Kansas City and would walk if she could go no other way. The men laughed indulgently at her fearless words, but I knew my mother meant what she said, and, when another and another day passed and still no mention had been made of breaking camp, I was not surprised when she awoke me early one morning and told me to dress quickly, as she and I were going to walk to Council Grove. Council Grove being the next stop on the Santa Fé Trail.

She then awoke Will and told him he must stay and take care of our things at the wagon. Before the sun arose or before anyone was stirring around the camp at Diamond Springs, mother and I made our way afoot out to the Santa Fé Trail. Autumn was coming and there was a tang in the early morning air. The hazel furze was yellow; there was the buff of honey-suckles and the violet of passion flowers. This was a different world from that of New Mexico with its dim distances and long silences. We walked for a time in silence. All that I thought of was the warm bed I had left in the wagon. I wished that mother had left me to guard the wagon and taken Will with her.

When we had walked for perhaps a mile and the prairie sun was painting the eastern sky crimson, we saw a man coming. He was riding a mule and jogging slowly. Remembering the tales of the Border Ruffians, mother drew me aside into a hazel thicket. We watched the approach of the lone rider; if mother was scared she did not show it. The man was funny and I saw mother smiling. She stepped out into the road beside him. The mule shied quickly and only the man's long legs prevented his sliding off behind. They were like scissors that clamped the mule's hindquarters as if to sever them from the mule's body. The man was tall and gaunt with an iron-gray beard. Long iron-gray hair hung from beneath his slouch hat. His long, thin face was lined with laughter wrinkles and his close set eyes were amused eyes. He carried a long rifle and was riding bare-back.

Mother asked him demurely if he were a Border Ruffian. "No, I ain't," he snapped back at her, "' I ain't no Ruffian of any kind." Then he asked us where we were going so bright and early, why we were walking and where? When mother told him about the camp at Diamond Springs and how frightened the wagon master and driver were, he threw back his head and broke into cackling laughter. "If it ain't jest like some little hundred-pound woman to put a bunch of men to shame," he said. "Now I own that place at Diamond Springs," he said, "and I aim to throw that bunch of cowards right out on their noodles. I'm going to find out what in tarnation they mean a house breakin'. I'll hev' the law on 'em and the United States Government. See if I don't." Then he added, kindly, "Little woman, you run right along. There ain't no Ruffians 'tween here and Council Grove. Ain't nothing between here and there but a passell o' Kaw Indians, and they are too lazy to hurt you or anybody. Besides they are scairt, if you say 'boo' to em." With that he was off down the Santa Fé Trail and mother and I walked on toward Council Grove. Looking back I watched the old man herding the mule down the trail with both his feet and long dangling legs. Someway as I watched him I thought of Yankee Doodle, who came to to town riding on a mule.

Council Grove was sixteen miles from Diamond Springs, and we halted only once and that was to eat our lunch in the shadow of a ruined water wheel. The trail forded a little stream near us, and while we sat there a mule splashed into the stream and stopped for a drink. On its back rode a woman man-fashion without a saddle and she carried a heavy basket on her arm. Mother said, "Has the world began riding mules, I wonder?" I rested and slept for a moment, my head on mother's spread-out dress skirt. When she awoke me it was with some tenderness. "We walk on now, my baby." She steadied me as I walked on beside her.

69

We saw no Kaw Indians to say "boo" to, neither did we meet a Border Ruffian. Long before we reached Council Grove I had forgotten both Indians and Ruffians. All that I could think of was how tired I was, and how hard it was to keep up with my mother, who evidently wanted to reach Council Grove before night came and caught us. I tried hard to be as brave and as uncomplaining as my mother, but the muscles in my slender thighs were twitching with fatigue when we climbed the steps of the store at Council Grove. When the grocery-man there asked me kindly if I was tired, I remember how I burst into tears and how mother had to answer him for me. We stayed that night in the home of the grocery-man where his wife put us to sleep on a great feather bed. As I dropped off to sleep that night I found myself wondering if all the beds in Heaven were not duplicates of the grocery-man's big feather one.

Mother awoke me early next morning. The Big Silver Dipper still hung in the mid-night blue of the heavens. I saw it as I drew on my shoes and stockings. But mother said we must hurry, a westbound wagon train was embarking. The driver who rode in a nice top-buggy said we might ride back to Diamond Springs.

I shall never forget that ride in my first top-buggy. Behind a team of dappled, spanking grays we out-distanced the slow moving wagons. As we covered the weary miles our feet had stumbled over the day before, I began building castles in the air. When I grew up, I said to myself, I would travel endlessly back and forth over the Santa Fé Trail. I loved the trail and would live always on it. I would travel always in a red-wheeled buggy like the wagon master's, behind a team of spanking grays. I would sleep every night on a great feather bed like the grocery-man's. I also would like a pink dress and a red rose for my hair. These were the dreams of my childhood ... but I still would like the buggy ride, and the red rose would not go badly.

"Yankee Doodle" had routed our wagon caravan from its comfortable quarters. We met them coming, and mother was able to tell the wagon master that she had broken trail as far as Council Grove; that there were no Ruffians to hurt him. I also remember that for days I was stiff and sore from my long pilgrimage. My life as I look back seems to have been lived best in those days on the trail.

Slowly the red oxen moved onward and the stately wagon followed as if impelled by the white sails behind them. The end of the trail drew nearer and nearer. One day the smoke of Fort Leavenworth could be seen ahead of us. A cheer went up from the drivers. I think both Will and I regretted that we had come to the end of the trail. We had loved the feel of the grass under our feet and the sound of the wind and the waters. The trail had been our point of outlook upon the universe. The blue sky above us had been bread and meat for our soul. If you have ever followed the old trail over mountains, through forests, felt the sting of the cold, the oppression of the heat, the drench of rains and the fury of winds in an old covered wagon you will know what I mean.

It was late in November before mother got us in school in Leavenworth. This time she sent me to a Young Ladies Seminary that was conducted by a Presbyterian minister, the Reverend Luther. Mother had said, "I want you to go to a Protestant school this time. You must not grow lop-sided in a religious way. You have received training under the Catholics, now I want you to go to a Protestant school. When you are grown-up you may choose for yourselves."

I was far enough advanced to attend the classes taught by Reverend Luther himself. The lower grades were taught by Mrs. Luther. Reverend Luther was a tall, lank man with a quantity of fair hair combed down on each side of his face that made his long features seem longer still. At recess the pupils from both rooms would play together, watched over either by Reverend or his small, fat dumpling of a wife. The green lawn sloped down to a white picket fence and here we gathered to play in a rough and tumble fashion at recess.

71

One game that we loved was leap frog and the leapingest little frog of us all was, Zeraldi. Sometimes today I seem to feel the grasp of Zeraldi Mimm's hands on my shoulder; feel her warm, little body go hurtling over me. In later years Zeraldi became the wife of the notorious Jesse James. When newspapers all over the land were recounting, the wild, bad deeds of that Jesse, my heart would ache for his wife. Zeraldi was younger than I, and attended the class taught by Mrs. Luther. I remember how Mrs. Luther, like a small, setting hen, would come fussing when the leap frog got out of bounds and was threatening to come up with a broken head or an arm.

Brother Will did not enter school this year. It was necessary that he help mother a bit with the living. Will was a big boy now. He was past thirteen, he said, and going on fourteen. He obtained employment in the newspaper office of the Leavenworth Times. The editor of that paper was Colonel Anthony, brother of Susan B. Anthony. Colonel Anthony became interested in my studious brother and did much to help him carry on his education. Will said that Colonel Anthony told him that if one would always work a little harder and with determination and intelligence, no goal was too high for him. Always Will had taken a more than normal interest in religion, although he had not been content to become a Catholic. Yet I do remember how he was always repeating some of Father Lamy's inspired words.

Now Colonel Anthony loaned him some sacred books of the East. They seemed to hold him enthralled. While I was drawing a well-remembered church with twin cupolas on the margin of my speller, and decorating it round about with strange likenesses of the Virgin, and crucifixes, and rosaries without number, Will was bent over the deep, old Eastern books. I remember how concerned the Reverend Luther became about my soul when he discovered some pictures I had drawn on the fly leaf of my big geography. It seemed that Catholic pictures had a way of fluttering out of my books at most unfortunate moments. The Reverend's agreeable light

72

gray eyes had a way of stopping me when I was drawing my pictures and then he would make me stand by my place and recite with him the "Lord's Prayer."

Many a sermon did my eleven-year old ears hear that held no meaning for them. My brain grew bewildered. I could not understand where and how I had strayed. I only knew that the church with the twin cupolas was dear to me and that I was more than homesick for the black-robed sisters. I would that I were back again to walk old Santa Fé's dusty streets.

Will's brown head in the evenings was always bent over his books. When mother would ask him to do anything around the house, he would raise his head, fretfully look at her with unseeing eyes, and say, "Let Sis do it." I felt abused, but mother seemed to get Will's point of view and, more than often, I did it. Unconsciously Will was preparing himself for the ministry. It was to be his chosen life's work. I had always hoped that at the end of his life of toil and sacrifice he saw the thing that he, as a child, had prayed for . . . his Saviour's face.

Not long after our return to Fort Leavenworth mother received a telegram saving that her mother who lived in Orangeville, Ohio, was dying. The message said, "Come at once." Mother and I made ready for another steamboat ride up the Mississippi. This time our boat was a stern-wheeler called the "Florilda." It, too, resembled a Dutch windmill in full motion. Mother and I were no sooner aboard than a darky began running about among the passengers saying, "All those who have not paid their fares, please step up to the Captain's office and do so." He made quite a merry song of it and pretty soon I was following him up and down the deck singing too. I have a vivid remembrance of the boat pulling out into the middle of the turgid stream and of hearing negroes singing from wharves along the bank.

On the deck was a dog with long unkept hair and sad eyes that seemed to be weeping. A man told mother the dog was a blood-hound and that he was used to catch

73

run away negroes. "Blood-hound" was a fearful name, and I managed to give the sad dog a wide berth as I followed the negro boy singing. When a man patted the dog on the head and called him a "good" dog I knew it could not be true. No good dog would chase negroes.

When we were half way to Orangeville the *Florilda* struck a snag in the river bed. Water began rushing in from a great hole in the bottom. The Captain hastily disembarked all his passengers on an island mid-stream. Then the little stern-wheeler was dragged out and repairs were in order. I remember how mother paced up and down on that island, impatient at the delay and anxious to be with her dying mother. I remember how the mosquitoes feasted on us and how a fire was kept going for relief from them. By the time we reached Orangeville death had preceded us.

A long, black coffin stood on trestles in the front parlor. Grandmother St. Clair lay there with her yellow hands folded, her wrinkled yellow face turned to the pillow as if sleeping. We had our breakfast in the kitchen and folks kept coming and going. They were all dressed in black like Catholic sisters, yet not one of them looked at me. Not one of them spoke to me. Something vital had gone from mother's face. Her wide eyes were grief-stricken. I laid my head down on the oil-cloth-covered table and wept. If this was death I wanted none of it.

I remembered the trappers on the Santa Fé Trail and how we had wrapped them in clean sheets and sung songs over them. I remembered how God had stood in the blue sky above us and held the two trappers in His arms tenderly. As I let the tears run down my small nose onto the oil-cloth-covered table I prayed, "Dear God, when I die let be out on the trail, under the blue, blue sky." Strange that I still find myself at times, repeating the prayer of my childhood. This conventional death where one sent yellow telegrams saying, "Come at once," and where folks went around all dressed in black without speaking or smiling, did not appeal to me; it still does not. Our trip back down the river was not a

74

happy one. There were hours at a time when little mother did not seem to know I was living. Of course I know now of what she was thinking.

Four years we spent in Leavenworth. For Will they were four studious ones for after the first winter he attended school, helping Colonel Anthony only in the evenings and on Saturdays. I carried on my work and became Reverend Luther's "little heretic." Once a year the school children were taken up the river on a picnic outing. I remember these picnics as the red-letter days of the year. They were a bit like the old days on the trail. I remember one place where we picnicked that a flock of snow-white geese waddled slowly across our picnic grounds. They were tame geese and had no respect for the snowy cloth we had spread on the grass. I remember one time we went in a wagon and the wagoner had some scarlet poppies in his hat. There would be a great wicker basket containing our lunch, and there would be Mrs. Luther, her broad face sweating under her brimmed hat.

I remember a cowslip ball the Reverend made for me, and how Zeraldi snatched it from me and tossed it right up in the middle of a tall willow tree where the crows had a nest. I remember how we all pelted her with the flowers we had gathered and how the Reverend smiled at us from his place where he stood guard over the picnic basket. I remember a farm that we visited and how the farmer took us to feed the doves, chickens and guineas. I remember how he let me feed a big ear of corn to a brindled cow, and how an old cat had five gray and white kittens up in a hay mow.

So four years went by in Leavenworth and I am eleven, then twelve, thirteen, fourteen and fifteen. Long years filled with the lust of young life and with growing. In the acquisition of more or less useless knowledge, soon to be forgotten, my childhood passed away.

A frequent guest in our home during this time was Reverend Leonidas Polk, who was, I believe, a distant relative of my father's. He was a graduate of West Point

75

and was consecrated missionary-bishop of Arkansas and the Indian territory south of the 36° 30', with provisional charge of the dioceses of Alabama, Mississippi, and Louisiana. He also had charges in the Republic of Texas. I think Will took him for a model. I know that he honored and loved him, and I think it was partly due to the Reverend Polk's influence that religion continued to be the guiding star of my brother's life.

I once heard Will telling Reverend Polk about our father's death at the Battle of Monterey, and of mother's long struggle with poverty. He told how our mother had given of her youth and her strength to keep her little family together. "Some day, please God," said Will, "I shall make it all back to her." Will's voice could be thrilling, solemn, proud and pathetic. It was a voice God-given. It was the voice of a preacher.

We did not lose touch altogether with our friends in Santa Fé. Though mail service by wagon train was slow, being months in transit, still letters did come and were read and reread by all of us. Sometimes Will and I would sit together under an elm tree in the side year letting our nostalgia run riot. We wondered if ever again we would see New Mexico with its Indians and Mexicans. We wanted another mess of goat meat seasoned with Mexican chile. We wanted to see the sisters, and go once more to the chapel . . . we wanted to go back west like so many of our elders.

CHAPTER FIVE

Back To New Mexico 1860

THE SPRING of 1860 found us still in Fort Leavenworth. It also brought to us the first, faint rumblings of civil war. We heard much talk of the Fugitive Slave Act, the Missouri Compromise, the Dred Scott Decision, and the John Brown Raid. Perhaps mother grew tired of hearing so much of the nation's unrest. Perhaps like Will and me, she was just homesick for the west. One morning when we three were eating breakfast at a small round table and Will and I were talking about the wonders of Santa Fé, she pushed her chair back quickly and stood up to say, "Keep still! I am as homesick as you are. I can stand no more of this talk of the plaza. We are going west again as soon as ever I can get passage in a wagon train for us."

Will and I whooped like Comanche Indians. We ate no more breakfast, for we were too happy. I remember saying that if I ever got back in sight of the mountains I would never leave. I was to discover that for many years, perhaps never, I was not to be master of my destiny. It seems I have always had to go where others led me. Even today I await in land not of my choosing. I wait, and as I wait, I keep thinking of that land of dim distance and long silence.

Mother said that perhaps this time we would go to Sutter's Fort stopping a while in Santa Fé, of course. We

77

secured passage this time in a large Government train of two-hundred wagons. The wagon master was a Mr. Hamilton. The train was sufficiently large that we did not feel much fear of the Indians, beside that Uncle Sam had been busy erecting forts along the trail. At these forts soldiers were stationed to protect the traveling public. By this time I felt quite grown-up for I was fifteen and Will was seventeen. I remember how he insisted on cluttering up our limited space with the heavy books he was bringing.

I also remember the light-heartedness of our start in the early dawn. Before noon two of the wagons, discouraged when they got out on the prairies, and by the fears of the women, turned back to Fort Leavenworth. When they turned back Will's eyes met mine and we both broke in to what I realize was heartless laughter. Confined to a mule's pace, as we were, with Fort Union two months before us, it never occurred to either of us that the trip would be boring or tiresome. We began at once looking for old camping places along the trail and would explain with delight when we came upon them. We drove with us a herd of horses and cattle and for that reason made haste slowly. Singing and shouting went on all about us. From a wagon ahead of us a violin was usually wailing. We traveled with order and system, in four great columns. When night came the outer columns drew in together while the inner two angled outward, wagon lapping wagon, thus making the round corral for the mules and the horses. The confident hilarity of the Santa Fé wagon trains is something to remember. The danger of Indians had lessened.

Sunday was a day of rest along the trail, unless perhaps, we had been held back by unexpected things. The wagon masters reasoned that the oxen, or horses traveled better and more willingly for that Sabbath day of rest. Religion occupied the mind of folks more in those days and God's Sabbath was not lightly violated. While I have no detailed remembrance of wayside services, yet I do remember the hymns that we sang around the eve-

78

ning camp fires. I also remember that we stood for a good-night dismissal in silent prayer. I remember with joy the spiritual blessing of a silent prayer beneath dark skies.

I was now old enough to help mother with the camp cooking and, since she had no boarders this time, she too, enjoyed the trip more. Sometimes I walked by the side of the wagon with Will and the driver. Frequently I sat by mother on the high spring seat of the wagon and crocheted diligently. I made four yards of fine, white lace to edge my someday-to-be bridal petticoat.

At last the brakes of the Missouri lay behind us and our white ships were sailing across the wide sea of grass. At Council Grove we spent the Sabbath. The grocery-man did not remember me, for I had grown tall. I wore a long dress, and braids of brown hair were coiled coronet fashion around my head. He did remember Mother the moment that he saw her alight from the wagon, and he came with both hands outstretched to meet her. We camped by the store that night and I remember how a Kaw Indian came and traded the grocery-man a shaggy red pony for a sack of white bolted flour. While we stood watching another Kaw came and the grocery-man traded him the pony for a buffalo hide filled with yellow Indian corn.

Next morning being the Sabbath we attended church services at the little meeting house. The preacher, a tall, young fellow, came and stood in the meeting house doorway. He welcomed his congregation; welcomed the weary travelers who had alighted from the covered wagons. He beamed upon us and ushered us to our places with, "the males sit on this side. The females over there." Will sat across the aisle from us. I remember how his eyes were alight to hear again the Word of God. He held his worn cap between his knees, his awkward hands moved restlessly. When the singing began Will forgot to be self-conscious and his lovely voice rolled out sweet and expressive in, "There is land that is fairer than day." When the tall, young preacher stood before us he

79

seemed at first at a loss for the proper words with which to express himself. The audience moved restlessly and then suddenly the words of the preacher began to glow. They were like bird's wings with the sunlight falling upon them. The little wayside meeting house was filled with strange pictures. Great beasts emerged from the shadows; death on a pale horse bore down upon us. Will's sensitive face glowed; his eyes were lambent. The preacher preached, prayed and exhorted. Heh eld his bible out before us. "This is the only book ever printed," he shouted, "that nas the power to heal a heart that is broken, or to make a good man out of a bad one." Before he dismissed us the Great Galilean came and held out His blessed hands to us. I can never forget the boy preacher, and I still marvel at the power that fell so strangely upon him.

When we neared the old house on the plains mother and I grew excited. What would we find there? Would the same lonely woman come to greet us? What about the little baby? That baby should be four years old now. When we drew near the place we realized that this time it actually was deserted. No sullen men loafed in shade there. Empty windows stared at us. A silence hung over the place. It was more dilapidated than ever. The sagging lean-to had fallen completely. But the caravan halted that water might be drawn from the well. It was Will who discovered the grave by the wire fence half-hidden by tumble weeds. A bit of weather beaten board with letters printed upon it told the meager story. "Sarah Grace Austin and infant daughter. October 24th 1856."

Before we reached Pawnee Rock a dozen Indians joined our cavalcade. They kept well in the rear, but would circle us at times to hoot and jeer at us. Perhaps they deemed it wise to keep us reminded of the old Pawnee Rock massacre.

The cabin where they had scalped the two trappers greeted us sadly, still untenanted, the traps hanging on the walls had grown rusty. The great double grave seemed unmolested. Will and I gathered flowers and placed them among the parasitic weed of the prairie called "love-entangle" that had covered the sunken grave with its golden beauty.

The buffalo were still numerous. Sometimes we had to take pains to avoid them. The country here was so level that we could see for miles in all directions and the sun seemed to come up or go down like a great yellow disk right into or out of the earth. Sometimes we heard a noise like thunder and then a great herd of wild horses would swoop past us. Wild horses were becoming quite common. They were descendants of horses the Indians had stolen from wagon trains along the Santa Fé and Oregon trails. Each herd was led by a stallion.

At Diamond Springs we found the old stone house sheltering a family of tow-headed Jayhawkers. Seven boys ranged up to watch our approach. They were like stair-steps ranging from a baby of two years to a hulking lad of fourteen. A level wheat field waved around the old sod corral. We caught no sight of "Yankee Doodle" or a Border Ruffian. Someone played a melodeon that night inside the rock house and sang, but we were not invited to help furnish the entertainment.

This trip across the plains we did not follow the Cimmaron Cut-off but went by the way of Raton Pass and Bent's Stockade. Bent's Stockade was a sort of gathering place for hunters and trappers. It was a bit like a present day country auction. A white man would hold up something he wanted to trade. The Indians would crowd around and do a lot of grunting. Then one of them would step forward and offer a blanket or a buffalo robe in exchange. The market for beads was not so brisk. The Indians now wanted guns and gunpowder. The more Indians present the better the trading, and for that reason there were always Indians lounging around Bent's Stockade.

It was here that some of our wagons left us to head northward. Gold had been discovered in the Pike's Peak region, and the gold excitement was running high. There was also a gold boom farther north on Cherry Creek, where the town of Denver was to spring into being.[21]

One evening at sunset we found ourselves on the banks of the Purgatoire River, where the town of Trinidad, Colorado, now stands. Our trail led us past a tall, white bluff where an Indian stood, tall and straight watching our wagons ford the river. Along the southern bank ran a buffalo trail, and a log *jacal* stood there among the brush and cedars.[22] The tall white bluff where the Indian stood we call today "Simpson's Rest," in honor of an old pioneer whose grave is there. The old *jacal* was replaced in later years by the Cardenas Hotel. Many adobe houses were to spring up along the trail where our covered wagons camped that evening in 1860. I remember how I lay that night and looked out across the shining ford of the Purgatoire river into the moon-drenched country across which we had traveled. I did not realize then that I would end my days in Trinidad beneath the tall bluff; that often when sleep defied me I would look at that same moon-drenched country and remember that camp of covered wagons.

Next morning while more than a hundred little breakfast fires were sending spirals of blue smoke heavenward, two Mexicans came from among the scrub cedar leading a little burro laden with venison. I remember how gladly we traded gunpowder for venison. We were not permitted to trade guns or gunpowder to the savage Indians.

Breaking camp while it was still early, our cavalcade began the steep and tortuous ascent of the Raton Pass. Today we glide easily over hairpin curves that in 1860 meant broken axles and crippled horses. The trail was a faint wheel mark winding in and out over fallen trees and huge boulders. Midday found us only a little way above the present site of Morley, Colorado. Our horses were jaded and tired, six of our wagons had broken axles. We made camp where a little icy cold spring bubbled by the wayside. We rested, ate and tried to repair some of the damage done to our wagons.

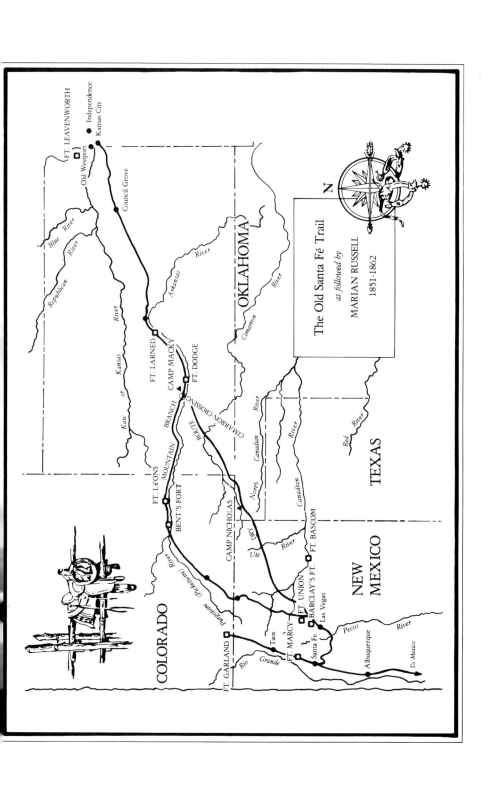

The Old Santa Fé Trail
as followed by
MARIAN RUSSELL
1851-1862

N

FT. LEAVENWORTH
Independence
Kansas City
Old Westport

Council Grove

Blue River
Republican River
River

Kansas River
Kaw or River

OKLAHOMA

Arkansas River

FT. LARNED
CAMP MACKY
FT. DODGE

MOUNTAIN BRANCH
ROUTE
CIMARRON CROSSING

Cimarron River

Red River

TEXAS

FT. LYONS
BENT'S FORT

CAMP NICHOLAS

North Canadian River
Canadian River

DRY
Ute River
FT. BASCOM

COLORADO

River
Purgatoire (Picketwire)

FT. GARLAND

Taos
FT. MARCY
Santa Fe
Rio Grande

FT. UNION
BARCLAY'S FT.
Las Vegas

NEW MEXICO

Pecos River

Albuquerque

To Mexico

ELIZA ST. CLAIR SLOAN
Mother of Marian Russell
From a tintype taken by Joseph J. Brown,
El Paso, Illinois, about 1855

ELIZA ST. CLAIR SLOAN
Mother of Marian Russell
Age 73
Photo courtesy of Pueblo, Colo. Library District,
E. M. Stringfellow Collection

MARIAN RUSSELL
Age 46
Photo taken at
the Hausman Studio, Trinidad, Colo. about 1891
Photo courtesy of Pueblo, Colo. Library District,
E. M. Stringfellow Collection

WILLIAM SLOAN
Who as a boy accompanied his sister, Marian Russell,
on the Santa Fe Trail
Senior Class photo, Rochester University, N.Y., 1869
Photo courtesy of Pueblo, Colo. Library District,
E. M. Stringfellow Collection

RICHARD D. RUSSELL
In dress uniform
Photo courtesy of Viola Russell

SONS OF MARIAN AND RICHARD RUSSELL
Right to left, George, Hal, Ollie, Ray
Photo courtesy of Pueblo, Colo. Library District,
E. M. Stringfellow Collection

MARIAN AND RICHARD RUSSELL'S SONS
Cutting hay on the family ranch, Stonewall, Colo.
Photo courtesy of Pueblo, Colo. Library District,
E. M. Stringfellow Collection

Next morning two covered wagons and a little herd of horses and cattle came down the trail from above us. It was a badly frightened German family traveling alone. The German told us how three men had joined his party several days before. One night he had inadvertently overheard them planning to murder his entire family for their wagons, horses and cattle. They had broken camp and come away, but the man was badly frightened. Mr. Hamilton, our wagon master prevailed upon the German to turn back with our caravan to Fort Union.

Always I remember the smell of the wild choke-cherry and the pungent odor of pine that greeted us that first morning. To our left lay what we call today "Fisher's Peak," but what we knew then as Raton Mountain. They said that great mountain side was infested with a specie of great, gray packrat, known no place else. The mountain was called by the early day Mexicans "Rat Mountain."

Once more we came to Fort Union and found Captain W. R. Shoemaker ordinance officer there. He was esteemed and respected by both the civilian and military population. His worth has been commemorated by naming the beautiful canyon on the Mora River east of Fort Union, Shoemaker Canyon, in his honor.

The soldiers had by this time so well accomplished their task that the frontier had been pushed back somewhat. The forays of the Indians in northern New Mexico were now only occasional. The next year, in 1861, Congress appropriated $35,000 for the improvement of the Santa Fé trail from Fort Union to Santa Fé through LasVegas. This was the first road-making of the west.

CHAPTER SIX

Land of Enchantment
1860-1866

FORT UNION had grown. There were more adobe buildings and better ones. I think mother would have liked to
have lingered there. I know that Captain Shoemaker
tried to induce her to stay and take some military boarders; however, she wanted to get Will and me enrolled in
school as quickly as possible so we pushed on to Santa
Fé.

I think I was never so glad to return to any place as I
was to Santa Fé that autumn of 1860. I brought with me
many eastern ways and a rather nice wardrobe. At
first I showed off a bit, but failing to impress either the
students or sisters, I forgot all about it and settled down
into my uniforms and the school routine as if I had not
been four years an easterner.

Mother moved again into the same house fronting the
Plaza, and soon had more boarders than she could well
handle. But this time there was no adjustment period
for us. We chatted with our Mexican neighbors in their
tongue. We cooked the hot chili and ate it. We shouldered the sleepy burros and sheep out of the way as we
walked down the narrow crooked alleys . . . alleys that
were ours by adoption.

Colonel Kit Carson came to see us in a new beaded
buck-skin jacket. He let us finger it and exclaim over its
beauty. The Indian women had woven porcupine quills

cleverly among the red beads. It was gorgeous. Many strange figures and designs were on that jacket, each an Indian symbol. The trousers were deeply fringed all down the outer legs and made him look like a chieftain. He came and sat on the settee by mother. They laughed together about the hold the land of the coyote and Indians had upon them. "It is rough I know, and maybe dangerous," said Mother, "but I love it."

While I started immediately to school at the convent, Will went with Colonel Carson and some wagoners to a salt lake located farther south in New Mexico.[23] Of his trip to the salt lake Will never tired of talking. How the lake was only a great snowwhite expanse of salt. How careful they were lest the Indians surprise them. When he returned he again enrolled in Bishop Lamy's school for boys behind the old church of San Miguel. Once more Father Lamy began trying to lay gentle hold on the heart of my brother. Sometimes I think that he must have been successful for always in the years that followed Bishop Lamy's name was held by my brother in reverence, even when he united with the Baptist church and became a missionary.

So life slipped back easily and quickly into the worn, old groove. Some of the girls I had known four years before had grown to womanhood and had left the walls of the convent. Some of the nuns had been sent to other schools and new sisters had taken their places. I remember how we day pupils ate our lunches in the little refectory in the side yard of the Academy. And how when the sisters left us for a moment we would all begin laughing and telling stories. The gossip we repeated was a bit different from the gossip in Leavenworth. One girl would whisper that while the Navahoes tried to be on good terms with the white folks, they were really spies and not to be trusted. Another one told of how an old Indian woman had stolen her mother's red mother hubbard right off the clothes line. Another girl whispered that the strangers in town, the ones with the wide leather belts and strange looking trousers and the spurs that

86

jangled, were Mexican guerrillas from old Mexico. One little girl told us that her mother had two little slave girls that were not worth their salt, and if any us knew anyone who wanted them her mother would be glad to give them away gratis.

One more happy year passed thus in Santa Fé, town of *manana*.[24] Then again mother conceived the idea of returning once again to Leavenworth. I really do not know why she wanted to go back but I think it was the lure of the trail that drew her. I know she loved Santa Fé and liked living there, but at heart my mother was a nomad. She gaily betook herself back and forth over the trail on first one pretext and then another. Who am I to condemn her, when today I would rather embark in a prairie schooner for parts unknown than to embark on white wings for a place in the skies called Heaven!

Sometimes today I am reminded of what the Indians told us about the scrub cedar—I think the cedar tree reminds me of mother. They said the cedar tree had power to close its branches on the approach of a snow storm, that way the snow fell only on the sides of the slender leaves. I have seen the cedar trees lifting up their boughs and turning the edges of their leaves to meet the falling snow. I have seen my mother lifting up her heart in an attitude of prayer that always helped her to bear what misfortune brought her. Today when I think of my pioneer mother I feel a joy unspeakable.

So once more we embarked in an eastern wagon train bearing cargo from far away California. Mule-drawn the wagons slid easily down to the cluster of huts on the Purgatoire. Many houses had sprung up there like little mud-colored mushrooms. There was a frontier store and a quaint Catholic church. We forded the river and camped this time on the northern bank beneath the tall, white bluff.

While we loitered around the fires that evening an old Mexican, wearing the tattered remains of a sombrero, slouched beneath the taut ropes of our wagon-corral and came toward us. He told us that the cluster of mud huts

87

was called Trinidad, and the river was called the Purgatoire. The early Spaniards had called it El Rio de las Animas Perdidas en Purgatoris, the River of Lost Souls in Purgatory. When we asked him why it was so-called, he said that many moons ago a tribe of cruel Comanches was forced by the Great Spirit to live forever beneath the surface of the earth, never again to see the light of day.

The old Mexican believed the Indian myth of the lost Indian tribe because there were places along the river where one might still hear strange sounds like the moans and curses of a people in pain. I remember how Will and I smiled at the story told by the old Mexican. In later years I was to be perplexed myself at hearing strange sounds like moans and curses coming from beneath the earth at places along the banks of the Purgatoire.

Even a year had wrought a change along the trail. We found a bit of plowed land here and there, black strips transversing our sea of silver grass. The Indians were there but so was the white man. The Indians were losing their fight. On the plains of Kansas the white men were killing the buffalo, killing them ruthlessly and in great numbers. The Indians stood sullen and resentful, watching the slaughter of their great herds.

This time mother moved to Kansas City. Once more I entered school, and Will found employment on the Kansas City Journal. He spent all his spare time that winter studying for the ministry. In the spring he united with the First Baptist Church. However, when Civil War came upon us he joined a Kansas regiment and marched away to war. I well remember the evening he came home dressed in his army blue. He paused a moment on the threshold tossed up his cap and shouted, "Hooray for Abe Lincoln." He spent a few days at home with us before he was sent away with his regiment. I remember how he smiled at us and how mother tried to keep smiling. I tried to take my cue from them, and the last morning I stood beside mother as Will was leaving. I stood very straight and returned smile for smile while I wondered if I would ever see my brother come marching

88

back again. Had we known, Mother and I, that we were not to see him again for fifty long years, perhaps we would not have been able to keep up the smiling.

Before those fifty years were ended Will was to have fought through the War, been ordained a Baptist minister, sent as a missionary to Calcutta, India, and then sent as a minister to Mexico City, Mexico.

He was stationed in Mexico City when that place was stirred by a great religious riot. With his own hands he rang the first Protestant church bell in that city. Later he was ordered back to the States. Finally Will did the thing that surprised us all. He renounced the Baptist Church and united with the Catholic Church. He never in after years discussed his strange conduct. I cannot explain to you what I never understood myself. Will was always honest and sincere. Religion was the guiding motive of his life. Perhaps the seed planted by Father Lamy in his heart so long ago had born fruit at last. Always I remember his childish prayer, "Please God, may I some day see your face."

I began putting my hair up in curl papers at night so that three shining curls might hang down over my shoulder next day. Gone were the blue pinafores and long brown braids. I was a young lady. In my dresser drawer was a small vial labelled, "The Bloom of Youth." Secretly I encarmined my lips and my cheeks with it, and dusted my face with rice powder. Sometimes I applied a black beauty patch near the corner of my mouth. They were supposed to be fetching. I laced heavy stays over fine white muslin underwear and carefully arranged my fly-away hoops and big padded bustle. My petticoats were wide and flounced, and I had a taffeta one for Sunday. My ball dress was wide and caught up at intervals with bunches of artificial tea roses. My hats were small and flower-laden. My parasol was smaller still. On my hands I wore silk half-handers.

Mother had great expectations. Although she was home sick for Santa Fé and the old trail she was determined to stay in Kansas City until I should marry well.

There was no one with a future out west, so she said. She encouraged many people to come to our home and the evenings were almost literary events.

A tall young man with dark commanding eyes came there one evening. He carried Harriet Beecher Stowe's newest book "Dred" under his arm. The young man's name was Gerald Roberts, and he read "Dred" aloud to us that evening. Gerald was in the mercantile business and was of superior financial and social standing. Perhaps mother could be forgiven for having encouraged his visits. I remember how flustered I was when his dark eyes rested long upon me. He was not long asking my hand in marriage. It was long ago, but I remember him standing holding my hand in his saying, "Miss Sloan, will you do me the honor to become my wife?" I stuttered and stammered and said, "Ask mother." The ring that he gave me was a diamond and I liked the feel of it on my finger.

I thought mother looked relieved, and I was a bit hurt when she said, "After your wedding, I think I shall go west again." Go west without me? Such nonsense! The days that followed were most unhappy with mother planning my wedding with the left ventricle of her heart, while she used the big right one to plan going out west. Sometimes I would take off the hoops and the bustle, and then I would remove the diamond and lay it upon them. No one would want to wear diamond rings and hoopskirts in an old covered wagon.

Spring came. It was 1862 and mother was going to Santa Fé. I was supposed to stay in Kansas City with Gerald who would soon be my husband. I just couldn't stand it. One evening I followed Gerald out on the stoop to say a good night and good bye forever. I left the ring with him and turned away from the hurt in his eyes to go tell mother that I was surely going to Santa Fé with her. For the first time she seemed disgusted. "I have tried so hard to do well by you," she muttered. Dear Mother! She did better by me than she dreamed when she let me go with her.

We missed Will sadly on this fifth trip over the trail. There have been many things in my life that I have striven to forget, but not those trips over the trail. The lure the old trail held for us. Seems that folks who made those trips in covered wagons never forgot them. I know an old pioneer who in 1846 went out over the Oregon Trail. He was eight years old when he started and ten years old when he reached the gold fields of Oregon. He died when he was seventy-seven. They said the day of his passing he had lain for hours without moving or speaking. Then suddenly he opened his eyes and said clearly, "Listen, I hear the rumble of the great covered wagons. Can you not hear how the wagons creak and groan as they fall into line? Hark! The drivers are singing. They sing as they walk by the oxen, 'The Oregon Trail, the Oregon Trail, the Oregon Trail' ". Michael, the old pioneer, sang as he lay dying.

That was the way it was. The lure of the old trail held for us. There was another tale of a pioneer trail, the trail that was called, "The Medicine Road of the White Man." An old woman told me about that trail and a child that she called Tessie. This is a tale of the prairies long ago. It is about fairies and angels and a little sod house by an emigrant trail.

"My father," said the old woman, gathered bones for a living. He gathered the bones of the bison, the wild mustang and the prong horned antelope. Old bones brought $5.00 per ton. They were used as fertilizer. Sometimes five ton was all the old bones my father could gather from one year's end to another. Did you know that a family of seven, nay eight counting Tessie, could live for a year on twenty five dollars and a handful of produce from a dry farm? Well they can if they have to!

"My father," said the old woman, "was Michael. The same Michael who sang as he lay dying. One day Michael was gathering some cow chips by the Medicine Road of the White Man. I was with him. So also were my brothers and my sister. That was the day we found the little waif that we called Tessie. She was asleep by the

91

old emigrant trail. She was a child of perhaps five years and she was lost or she had been abandoned. She must have been suffering from hunger and thirst, yet she was afraid of us and she struggled in father's arms when he carried her home to Martha, my mother.

"Martha took one look at the strange wild creature struggling in father's arms and then she dropped to her knees and held out her arms. Tessie stood for a moment poised on one dirty foot and then, straight as a homing pigeon she went into mother's arms, into mother's heart of love, and there she stayed and there was nothing we could do about it. Mother adored her and that was all there was to it.

"Tessie stayed with us in the sod house for perhaps a year and during that time she never spoke to any of us. She never laughed and she never cried, for Tessie was deaf and dumb. Sometimes when she was greatly excited, like the day the dryland terrapin crawled in at the sod house door, she would go and lay her thin little face against mother's arm and break into a queer twittering like the cry of some wild bird. That was the only sound she ever uttered. She fluttered around the sod house like a great yellow butterfly, for her hair was a tawny yellow and her enormous eyes were the color of amber. She was a strange elfin-child half fairy. Always there was a touch of other-whereness about her. Sometimes she would stand with her head on one side as if listening to the sounds of music from far away.

"Tessie was about my age," said the old woman, "and willingly did I share with her my wee calico dresses, my flour sack underwear and my little trundle bed. But a place in my mother's heart was an entirely different matter. I grew jealous of Tessie. One day I said bitterly, 'Mother, why do you love her? I am a lot smarter than she is.' Tessie turned her great startled eyes upon me and mother said quickly, 'Nay 'tis not true. Tessie is smarter. She has been touched by the angels and lives her life apart. Can you not see how she seems to be always listening? Some day a voice will call. An unseen

92

hand will beckon and our Tessie will go away. We must be very good to her.'

"There came then a night when moonlight lay white on the prairies. Mother awoke from a long sleep to find Tessie standing in the door of the sod house. She was wringing her thin little hands and uttering her queer bird-like twittering. Mother arose and put her back into the bed with me and tucked her in and after awhile Tessie grew quiet. I put my arms around her and resumed my own slumber.

"When the morning came Tessie was not in the trundle bed with me. She was sitting on the floor by mother's bed. Her little round head with the tightly braided pigtails was resting on the pillow close by mother's own, but Tessie was dead. The voice had called, the unseen hand had beckoned and Tessie had gone away. One little hand still rested on the rag carpet. The other was reaching toward mother.

"Whence came the child, Tessie? We never knew for the old emigrant trail kept its secret well. She sleeps tonight on an old limestone hill close by Martha's side, finding in death all that she had ever asked in life, proximity to mother's heart of love."

When I think of the Santa Fé trail I think of my own mother, and how she was never quite happy unless she were passing back and forth over it . . . or planning to.

In later years she was at last enabled to go out to California, the end of the rainbow! She found there the gold of peace and plenty. Her life ended there and she sleeps today by the waters of the blue Pacific.

While this trip of 1862 was my last trip over the Santa Fé trail, it was not mother's last one. She made several trips after I was married to Lieutenant Russell and settled down in New Mexico. On one of these trips she had an experience that is worthy of recounting.

She had engaged passage in the wagon train of one Captain Feltz in whose wisdom and experience she felt confidence. The eastward bound wagon was not heavily loaded. The wagon in which mother rode had a Mexican

93

driver and Mr. Feltz gave it place in the caravan next to his own lead wagon. Mother slept in the wagon and the driver slept beneath it.

Since mother had money stolen on our first wagon trip westward she had taken more precautions. This time she had a small cloth bag containing her money pinned in the front of her dress. At night she would place it deep down in the corner of her pillow slip. She really was a seasoned old trail traveler and not given to nervous fears about her safety; however she had never liked the appearance of the surly Mexican driver. Captain Feltz had taken him on in Santa Fé when one of his own wagoners had fallen ill and could not make the trip.

One day when mother dressed she forgot to remove the bag of money from her pillow. When she thought about it later in the day she climbed back among the bedding, found the bag and was pinning it in the bosom of her dress when she looked up and saw the surly Mexican watching her. Several times that afternoon she found him watching her furtively. Once she thought of telling Captain Feltz that she was frightened, but was ashamed of her cowardice. That night the moon shone brightly through the wagon's white cover. Mother lay awake and listened to the sound of the wind, and wondered why she could not hear the driver snoring beneath her.

At the front of the wagon the canvas cover was drawn taut and tied with a small rope like a draw-string. It seemed to mother that the sheet vibrated and it was accompanied by a slight rustling sound. It was that hour of the night when velvet-footed animals are wont to prowl, but the rustling sound seemed to come from close at hand. She lifted herself quietly in bed until the knotted rope was almost within reach of her hand. She saw a black, misshapen shadow outlined against the white canvas wagon cover. The moonlight glittered on a long sharp knife. Suddenly the rope was severed and the wagon cover was flung open. The surly Mexican slid sinuously into the wagon with her. Mother's echoing scream sent him scrambling back over the tongue of the wagon. It also brought Mr. Feltz running.

Next morning the men of the train held tribunal. The Mexican was questioned and he confessed that his motive was murder. He said that he had seen mother putting the money in her dress. He said that he planned to scalp her and that the men would perhaps think some prowling red skin was guilty.

Mr. Feltz decided the wagon train would move onward without the Mexican driver. To be set adrift alone on the Santa Fé trail was a punishment sometimes meted out to malefactors. When the train pulled out next morning he was left sitting disconsolately by the side of the trail. Perhaps some other train would pick him up, or, perhaps, the Indians would find him and complete his well-deserved punishment. Nothing was ever heard from him.

This year romance drew her shining skirts across the door of the Academy at Santa Fé. A Captain Grayson, who had been stationed at Fort Union, was ordered to the Civil War front, and, for that reason sent his young wife, a bride of one month, to the convent at Santa Fé for protection. Mrs. Grayson was a pretty girl about sixteen years of age. She worried a great deal about her husband, for week after week went by and she did not hear from him. I remember her during those weeks of waiting as a quiet child with great eyes set in a small pale face.

After she had been with us at the Academy for about six weeks word was received that her husband had been killed in action. For awhile she was ill, and the students and sisters vied with each other trying to please her. For two years she stayed on at the convent, as that seemed to be the only home that she had. Sometimes she helped with the teaching. One day a young rancher whose name was George Hebert passed by on his way to the plaza and saw Mrs. Grayson on the lawn of the Academy. It was a case of love at first sight with George Hebert. Men did really fall in love in those days and women were really shy and timid.

95

Courting a girl shut up in a convent is uphill work, and has seldom proved successful. However, young Hebert was persevering. His ranch, the now famous Glorietta estate, was situated some distance southeast of Santa Fé. It was sadly in need of the guiding hand of a woman. George Hebert went and laid his troubles before Father Lamy. George had a reputation of honesty and sterling worth in the community and Father Lamy knew this. He made himself a kindly ally in Cupid's campaign. Some way a meeting was arranged outside of the walls of the convent and at that first meeting they were married. Their honeymoon, and, in fact, the remainder of their lives, they spent at the ranch at Glorietta. They were always happy and always in love with each other. Mrs. Hebert and I were about the same age, and, as the years passed, we saw more and more of each other.

Once, on a birthday, Mrs. Hebert sent me a book for a present. I still have it. It was called Society Salads. It contained besides recipes many beauty hints. I remember that it said drinking coffee made a young lady's complexion most sallow. Buttermilk tossed together with tansy and spread over the face at night would remove tan and sunburn. Society Salads also reminded us that perfect ladies seldom had healthy appetites. It said that delicate ladies fainted easily, and that they never, never chewed gum. It explained how one might faint without any trouble and without damage to dress or deportment.

After school closed in June of the year 1864 we moved to Fort Union. We lived in a long, low adobe house whose six rooms were all in a row. The eastern room of that house we rented to the Masons for a lodge room. The Masonic Lodge in Fort Union was organized in that year.[25] There was much talk and argument about using a room on the ground floor of any building for a Lodge room. However, there were no upper stories in Fort Union. Special permit was obtained from the mother lodge in Missouri to use the ground floor as a lodge room.

96

They tell me the Fort Union Lodge, still in existence at Wagon Mound, New Mexico, uses that special permit, and the lodge room is still on the ground floor. I remember the discussions that we had pro and con when Colonel Kit Carson applied for membership. His wife, "little Jo" was a Catholic, and he had been married within the Catholic Church; yet he did become a member.

The first altar cloth my mother made for the Masons was made from a fragment of one of Bishop Lamy's robes. That cloth had come all the way from Leavenworth by ox team. In those days factory woven cloth was precious, and when one had a yard or more left over from the making of a garment, they were permitted to put it back in store at Santa Fé for reselling. Thus it was that mother bought the beautiful remnant on one of her trips to Santa Fé and from it made the altar-cloth. I am told that old altar-cloth is preserved at Wagon Mound today. It is under glass on the wall of the Masonic Lodge there. I believe that in the beginning the Fort Union Lodge was called Chapman Lodge in honor of Colonel William Chapman.

The Civil War did many things to Fort Union. Many of its officers went into the southern Confederacy, but the majority did not. Some time after the close of the war Chapman Lodge was partially destroyed by fire. It is said that a part of the old furnishings were moved to Las Vegas and a part to Wagon Mound.

It was at Fort Union in the year of 1864 that I first met Lieutenant Richard D. Russell. I was rounding a corner rather suddenly, my green veil streaming out behind me. The wind was blowing my hair in my eyes and I was trying to keep my long skirts where they belonged when suddenly he stood before me. That was the moment the whole wide, world stood still. My tall, young lieutenant stood and smiled at me while I struggled with my skirts, veil and hair. Then on he marched with his company, taking my ignorant young heart right along with him. For days the memory of his smile came

97

between me and my prayers. Almost immediately he made an opportunity to be formally presented. Mother, it seemed to me, found many occasions to compare my lieutenant unfavorably with Gerald Roberts. Love, they say, is like the measles: We take it only once. Cupid spends no second arrow on our hearts. I am sure that was true in my case, for from that August day when I met Richard on the streets of old Fort Union, to that other August day twenty-three years later when an assassin's bullet took him from me, my love never faltered. Indeed, that love is a living part of the soul of me today, although the grass has waved over my lieutenant these forty years and more.

Richard was born in Canada in 1839. He was six years older than I. One evening he sat in our house at Fort Union and told mother and me about his adventurous life. Mother said she knew that evening that Richard had fallen in love with me. He told her how his parents had been visiting relatives in Canada when he was born, and how he had always regretted the fact that he been born outside the United States.

When he was sixteen, Richard, in company with another young boy, ran away from his father's home in Illinois, and wandered west with an emigrant trail to California. That was in the year 1855. He said that he would never forget the long, hard trip across the lava beds of the Indian Country and Arizona, for like all boys he had walked most of the way beside the driver.

Reaching California he had sought first the gold fields but had no luck finding the elusive yellow metal. So he obtained employment on a cattle ranch. As soon as he was old enough, he homesteaded on the Sacramento River. He built a cabin there and several miles of stake-and-rider fence to hold his little herd of Texas longhorns.[26] About that time war drums began sounding, and Richard sold his little ranch and enlisted with the First California Volunteers. Richard was always a pioneer, and not a soldier at heart. He loved the wide open spaces and liked pulling up stakes and moving westward

98

a few jumps ahead of civilization. The old pioneers were a restless lot of nomads; yet they watered the seeds of freedom with their own hearts blood.

The First California Volunteers were ordered immediately to New Mexico, where General Carleton was having a bad time with the Indians.[27] The Confederates were, at that time, holding Albuquerque, and they were inciting the Comanches and Apaches to deeds of horrible violence. The coming of the First California Volunteers forced the Confederates to evacuate Albuquerque and retreat southward. General Carleton was then able to turn to the hostile Indians. Arizona was then embraced in the territory called New Mexico. It was a dreary, thirsty land of 20,000 whites and 40,000 Indians. The whites kept together near the forts, and were always more or less in terror when it was necessary to leave the forts' protection. Scarcely a day passed that we at Fort Union did not hear of some fresh Indian outrage or massacre.

When September rolled around, mother moved again to Santa Fé. I was sick at heart because so far she had never permitted Richard and me a moment alone together. Always we were chaperoned; always mother or some elderly couple was with us. Only our eyes could speak of the dawning love in our young hearts.

We moved to Santa Fé and a whole week passed, and I had not heard from my lover. Then one morning a great caravan was sighted coming in from Fort Union. I thought surely there would be a letter for me from Richard so I dressed up a bit and walked to the post office. I stood waiting among the jostling throng until my turn came at the window. There was no letter for Miss Marian Sloan. No news from my tall lieutanent.

I recall that I had dressed with special care that morning. My dress was of factory-woven cloth, in what they then called cotton challis. It was a glorious dress of a soft golden color. It had a tight little bodice buttoned down the front with little jeweled buttons. The sleeves were long and close-fitting. At my throat was cream lace ruch-

99

ing and mother's cameo brooch. The skirt of my long dress had many fluttering ruffles. That day at the post office lies in my memory as faint and sweet as the scent of old lavender. I had turned sadly from the post office window and was starting homeward when some one came up behind me and drew my hand through his arm. I turned quickly. It was Richard. He had come with the emigrant train from Fort Union. My heart overflowing with joy, I went where he led me and soon we were standing beneath the great wooden arch on the outskirts Santa Fé. We were alone for the first time since the day of our meeting.

Eastward the wide trail flowed like a river. From the blue hills came the tinkle of sheep bells. It was the close of an Indian summer day; it was also the close of my girlhood. Standing for one brief forbidden moment within the circle of Richard's young arms I seemed to see a little girl with long brown braids dressed in a blue pinafore. I saw her standing before me, then she slipped away in the shadows along the trail. Little Maid Marian, as the soldiers at the Forts along the trail had called me for all the ten years they had known me, had slipped away among the shadows.

Six months from the day of our meeting Richard and I were married in the little military chapel at Fort Union; that was in February of 1865. I was twenty. Mother had sent to Kansas City for my trousseau. I still think it was very lovely. My wedding dress was of soft beige and fitted my slender figure. My hat, adorned with a single white feather, was small and turned away from my face at one side. My cape of blue velvet covered me from tip to toe. Such an elegant costume for a bride in New Mexico in the "sixties!"

I am afraid that I did not hear a great deal of our wedding ceremony, for something sacred and triumphant was going on in my heart. Somewhere on the hills of God, angels were singing; all the bells of Heaven were ringing. I heard Richard's deep voice beside me saying over and over, "I do" and "I do." Then all at once we were outside in the patio, and fine white snow was blowing little drifts in the folds of my new velvet cape. There were tears in mother's eyes, but Richard held my hand tightly. I was Mrs. Richard Russell.

From our wedding in February 1865, until May of that year, Richard and I lived in Fort Union. Our honeymoon in the old fort was a happy one. Our living quarters were next door to those of Colonel Carson's.[28] I was the only white woman in the fort and the soldiers made much of me.[29] I remember how some of the soldiers gave me their money on pay day and asked me to take care of it for them. They were all given to gambling.

Sometimes I would ride horseback around the fort, but never alone and never far distant. It was too dangerous. The Apaches were growing bolder and more and more cruel. The Comanches were driving off the white man's sheep and cattle. Emigrant trains were being cruelly harrassed.

These emigrant trains, flowing in a continual stream along the great artery of travel between the Mississippi River and the coast of California, required the protection of soldiers. Fresh water springs through New Mexico and Arizona were always twenty, and sometimes forty miles apart. To overcome this shortage of water a continuous line of military posts and a system of artesian wells were planned. Of the military posts thus planned Camp Nickols was the first to be built east of Fort Union. It was completed in June of 1865 and was abandoned in September of that same year.

In May after our marriage Richard was ordered to go and help in the building of Camp Nickols. Shocking massacre after massacre had taken place. Colonel Carson was getting frantic. Something had to be done to protect the long line of wagons that was pouring westward. He thought that a fort built somewhere along the New Mexico-Oklahoma line would answer the purpose. Camp Nickols was to be this fort. It was the policy of the Government to keep always in mind the permanent good of the white man while bestowing as many temporary indulgences upon the Indians as it could. The Cheyenne and Arapahoes had by this time added their forces to the Comanches and Apaches. Wagon trains no longer attempted to cross the plains without military escort. Three hundred soldiers were immediately stationed at Camp Nickols. The idea being that when four or five large trains had gathered there, a detachment of soldiers would escort them as far east as Fort Larned, in Kansas, and then wait at Fort Larned to escort westbound trains back to Camp Nickols or Fort Union.

Sometimes wagon trains were forced to wait several weeks at the forts for military escort. Just before Camp Nickols was built Colonel Kit Carson had become incensed over the massacre of five white persons at Cimmarron Springs, and over the theft of a great herd of horses from the wagon train of a Mr. Allison, who was California bound. These two events caused Colonel Carson, together with Major A. H. Pfeiffer, to set out eastward with their complements of wagons, cavalry, scouts and a band of cattle to look for the location of a new fort.

This location was found at the prong of a little stream called the Carrizo, meaning the Nameless. The little fort they built was named Camp Nickols and was located about 130 miles east of Fort Union.

Colonel A. H. Pfeiffer was one of the most noted Indian fighters of the southwest. During Colonel Carson's 1863-64 campaign against the Navahos, Pfeiffer led one hundred men through the Canyon de Chelly, driving the Indians before him.

Little Camp Nickols became in a jiffy as impregnable as an old castle. It was surrounded by rock walls and a deep ditch or moat. Inside the rock walls the houses were half-dugouts four feet under ground and four foot rock walls above ground. The only two-roomed house was used as a hospital. Mounted howitzers were placed along the walls. There were stone rooms outside the rock walls along the south side for the officers. A flag pole was placed near the entrance.

When Richard was ordered to Camp Nickols in May, I was determined to go with him. I knew that Colonel Carson would not think it was very safe, so I began planning on how I might get his consent. I asked him to come to our quarters and be guest of honor at a little dinner party. I knew he liked my cooking, which he said was just like my mother's. That evening I prepared the pot-roasted buffalo meat the way I knew that he loved, with the red chili pods mixed with it. He watched me and smiled gravely as I presided. I think that he saw through my little ruse, but enjoyed it. When our other guests had gone, he did not wait for me to broach the subject, but told me kindly and firmly it was no use coaxing. I can see him yet as he laid a kindly hand on my shoulder; I can hear his kindly voice saying, "I promised your mother I would look out for you, Marian. You are safer here than at Camp Nickols." He stood under the hanging coal oil lamp in our quarters, a slight man with a frown between eyes that showed an infinite capacity for tenderness. When he saw the tears that were gathering he said, "Little Maid Marian, believe me I will take you out to Camp Nickols as soon as it is safe for you there." Years later I was to go to the ruins of Fort Union and find the little roofless room where Colonel Carson had stood that May day refusing me the one thing on earth that I wanted.

By the middle of June 1865, Colonel Carson, true to his word came to get me. Richard came with him and a small detachment of soldiers. My trunk and personal effects were placed in an army wagon. I rode on a dappled gray mare beside Richard and Colonel Carson. The ride to Camp Nickols remains as clear in my mind today as the day I took it. Colonel Carson, his mind on the Indian atrocities, kept pointing out places where some disaster had occurred. When we came to the crossing of White's Creek he had me dismount and stand by a heap of stones with him. It was here that Indians attacked the wagon train in which the White family traveled. Mrs. White, her small daughter and a female slave were taken prisoners. When the Indians were overtaken by a force of white soldiers they killed Mrs. White, whose still warm body was buried here by the soldiers. Neither the little daughter nor the female slave were ever heard from.[30]

When we reached Camp Nickols no house had yet been finished. Several hundred army tents were being used as quarters. Colonel Carson had a tent erected next to his own for Richard and me. The weather was very warm, and we kept the sides of the tent rolled up to catch the stray breezes. So also did Colonel Carson, and I remember seeing him lying on his cot on hot afternoons scanning the countryside with a pair of field glasses.

One night a great thunderstorm came up. I had never known the wind to blow so hard. It came fitfully and in a circular motion. At intervals the lightning would tear jagged holes in the black sky and our tent would be illuminated with an unearthly blue light. Suddenly our tent pole buckled. I hid my head under Richard's arm and did not hear Colonel Carson calling. Richard was trying to find his clothing when the Colonel's cry changed suddenly into a roar of rage. His tent had fallen down upon him. Richard had to call out the Corporal of the guards to get the Colonel extricated.

During Colonel Carson's brief stay at Camp Nickols, I saw little of him, for he seemed always busy. He personally directed the construction of the officers' quarters, and often he would ride out with the scouts and be gone all day. Each morning ten scouts would ride out on the prairies. They would return in the evening. Two pickets were kept posted during the daylight hours. They were mounted on the fleetest ponies. Other sentinels were placed at strategic places along the trail. Colonel Carson's vigilance never relaxed for a moment.

Colonel Carson did not seem extra well those days at Camp Nickols. I think the army rations did not agree with him. Some days his face seemed haggard and drawn with pain. The disease that was to claim his life in later years had even then fastened itself upon him.[31] I remember that he liked to play seven-up with the officers, and when they were playing I often heard his short, sharp little bark of laughter.

One morning the Colonel came leading his big black horse by the bridle. "Little Maid Marian," he said, "I have come to say Good-bye." His last words to me as he rode away were, "Now remember the Injuns will git ye if you don't watch out." I watched him as he rode away. The picket on the western lookout arose as he passed and saluted. The black horse mingled with mirage on the horizon and thus it was that Kit Carson rode out of my life forever. I was destined never to see his face again.

Richard and I did not live long in a tent. A nice dugout was soon made for us. It had a dirt floor and a dirt roof. The door was an army blanket. Our bed was some cedar boughs, nice and springy. We had a folding army table and two folding camp stools.

I really had no work to do and I read and reread every book and paper the camp afforded. Our mail was irregular, arriving from Fort Union by express, and by wagon train from the east.

A soldier was assigned us as cook. He prepared his savory stews on a Dutch oven outside as we had no stove. He carried water from the river in a great wooden bucket, and was always trying to cook something nice and special for me. Our bill-of-fare was monotonous: hard tack, beans, coffee, venison or beef. A beef herd had been brought from Fort Union, and the scouts killed both deer and antelope for us.

When a freight wagon arrived one day from Fort Union, Richard bought $42.00 worth of groceries and we ate the lot in ten days. A number two can of peaches cost us $2.00 and everything else was in proportion.

After Colonel Carson left, Colonel Pfeiffer was in command at Camp Nickols.[32] Some of the officers under him were Captains Kemp, Hubbell, Strom, Anderson, Drenner, Ortner and Richard. Perhaps Captain Strom was the best-dressed and most popular officer. I never remember seeing him, even on the warmest days without his uniform buttoned neatly and his military hat at a proper angle.

The camp boasted ten Indian scouts, two Indian squaws, and two Mexican laundresses. The laundresses were wives of two Mexican soldiers. Each soldier at Camp Nickols paid one dollar a month for his laundry.

The first detachment of soldiers sent out from Camp Nickols as military escort was under Captain Strom. The prairies around the camp had been covered with wagons, waiting for escort eastward. Captain Strom escorted them east as far as Fort Larned. When two weeks elapsed and Captain Strom did not return and more and more wagons were collecting, Richard was ordered to lead an escort eastward. He was to join Captain Strom at Fort Larned and return to Camp Nickols with him. Of course I was not permitted to go with him, although I thought that my dappled mare and I would have made a nice escort for anybody. I said Goodbye to Richard bravely, for I expected he would be back in two weeks yet it was more than a month before he returned to me.

I passed that lonely month as best I could without Richard. I took little walks around the fort, bearing in mind Colonel Carson's words, "The injuns will git ye if ye don't watch out." Sometimes I went to watch the Mexican women pounding dirt out of the soldiers clothing on the bank of the little Carrizo. Sometimes I watched the squaws tanning buckskin. They would smear the hides all over with the brains of the freshly slain animals, and then they would scrape and scrape them with small sharp pebbles. In time the hides became a soft, pliable white.

Major Pfeiffer, seeing how lonely I was, gave me riding lessons.[33] He taught me how to mount a horse properly and how to sit in the saddle. The Major was an elderly man crippled in one hip. It seemed that when he was stationed at Fort McRae, his wife and two women servants were killed by the Indians. Major Pfeiffer was in the bathtub when he heard a commotion. It was said that he came stark naked from that bath room and fought a defensive battle with a rifle. He was shot in the hip with an arrow.

One evening after Richard had been gone for what seemed to me like an eternity, I climbed up on top of the dugout and sat there watching the Santa Fé Trail which lay like a discarded ribbon flung eastward by a giant hand. The prairies lay bathed in the red sunset. My heart ached from days of weary waiting. As I sat there I saw a wagon train coming, many hundreds of wagons escorted by a detachment of soldiers. There were wagons drawn by mules, oxen and horses. There was a great herd of cattle. Soldiers rode in dusty ranks on either side of the caravan. Trembling I arose to my feet as the caravan drew nearer. A dusty lieutenant swept me a grand gesture at the gate of the fort. Lieutenant R.D. Russell had returned to his waiting bride in Camp Nickols!

There was another officer somewhat older than Richard in Camp Nickols, one DeHague, also a Lieut. He and Richard spent many pleasant hours planning on what they would do once they were mustered out of the army. They decided they would go in together in the mercantile business. I think that I never really liked DeHague, and looking back on those days at Camp Nickols the memory of the man DeHague is the only unpleasant one that I have.

In September of 1865 orders came from Colonel Carson to break camp at Fort Nickols and return at once to Fort Union. 'Tis an unforgettable picture I have of the morning we left the little camp on the Carrizo. We heard the soft, clear call of a bugle, the sound of marching feet. Infantry and cavalry fell quickly into formation, then passed out through the eastern gateway. When out on the trail they swung north, then west and hit the trail to Fort Union. There were army wagons laden with supplies and equipment; there were the loose horses and the remnant of the beef herd. Inside the stockade we left a great stack of hay and another one outside. The flag of the Union we left flying from the tall flag pole. On its base we posted a notice warning all persons against destroying Federal property. This was the official end of Camp Nickols.

No sooner had we reached Fort Union than Richard had orders to proceed to Fort Bascom, a small outpost on the Canadian River, in eastern New Mexico. All territory between the Red and the Canadian Rivers was called New Mexico at that time. To Fort Bascom we went. It was a picturesque place among low, rolling foothills. Here the officers' quarters, as at Fort Union, were made of logs, and arranged in a square around the parade ground. In the center of the parade ground stood a tall flag pole with Old Glory always waving.

That flag pole is associated in my mind with military discipline. The "California Walk" around that flag pole was a punishment meted out to offenders. Forced to carry on his shoulder a four-foot length of green log, the offender march around that flag pole from daylight until dark. One hour of marching was followed by one of rest. Sometimes a soldier would be sentenced to sixty days of the California Walk. I have seen as many as six soldiers doing the California Walk at one time. I think that it was called the California Walk by members of the First California Volunteers who had not forgotten the long days of forced marching from California to Albuquerque.

Sometimes, for what seemed to me trivial offences, soldiers would be suspended by their thumbs for hours at a time. Their feet would just clear the ground and the weight of their entire body would be upon their poor thumbs. An old German by the name of Pete Borden was one swung up by his thumbs. Hanging there by his swollen purple thumbs he begged a passing soldier to come wipe his nose for him. The soldiers seemed to think it a joke, but the stern military discipline seemed cruel to me.

For a time I was the only white woman in Fort Bascom; some miles above the fort, however, lived a white pioneer family by the name of Dorsett. Mrs. Dorsett was a jolly young woman with a red, round face. She had four little children all with tow-colored hair and small turned-up sun-blistered noses. I saw as much of Mrs. Dorsett as I could, for I was so lonely. Later I was to owe much to Mrs. Dorsett's skill as a mid-wife.

We had come to Fort Bascom in September of 1865 and my baby came in March of 1866. Because I was ignorant, I rode horse back up until the day of my baby's birth. Richard and I were dumb children embarked on life's greatest adventure.

On New Year's Day we decided to make a call on the Dorsetts. I rode my little dappled gray and Richard rode a huge strawberry roan that had just been sent up from the Navajo country. He was a wicked animal with a Roman nose and a touch of loco.[34] We set out quite gaily, and were scarcely out of sight of the fort when a demon seemed to take possession of the roan horse. I was only amused when the animal flashed past me with the bit in his teeth. I knew that Richard was an excellent horseman. But an unexpected thing happened. The locoed animal ran into a tree with full force. Richard was thrown from the saddle. His head came in contact with the tree and he lay as one dead. The big roan ran madly.

My dappled gray was doing her best to keep up with them, but when I saw Richard lying like one dead I had an impulse to slip from my saddle and see if I could not run faster. That is what I did but the long skirt of my riding habit tripped me. Suddenly the earth seemed enveloped in curiously fading twilight. I saw it coming up to meet me and I, too, lay unconscious in the road. How many precious minutes I wasted in my fainting, I do not know. I found myself at last looking up into the high, blue sky above me and wondering vaguely about a single white cloud floating there. When memory returned, I soon had Richard's head in my lap. It was bleeding. I tried vainly to stop the flow of blood with an inadequate handkerchief, believing all the time that he was dead. A government horse trader had seen the accident from his lookout on a distant hill, and he came galloping up to us. An ambulance was sent from the fort, but Richard had brain concussion and did not regain consciousness until the next morning. For many days he lay in the hospital. Three ribs were broken and he had an internal injury.

Some odd events took place at Fort Bascom. Once a Mexican laundress became deeply offended at something a white soldier was supposed to have said about her. She told the white soldier that if he ever told another lie on her she would cut his tongue out if it were the last thing she ever did. The man laughed at her. One day the soldier and the Mexican woman's husband got very drunk together. They went into the Mexican woman's quarters to sleep their drunk off. She managed someway to cut off the tip of the white soldier's tongue. Just how she managed it I do not know. But I remember that it happened after my baby was born. Richard and I owned the only cow in the fort. We had to divide her milk with the wounded soldier. He was in the hospital and could eat no solid food.

Convent raised, my knowledge of childbirth was limited. I really was not sure that I was to have a baby. I had no clothes prepared for its coming. One morning in March as I sang at my work in the kitchen, I was struck with a bolt from the blue. My baby was coming. They rushed me to the hospital where the young army surgeon was reduced to a hopeless wreck before my ordeal had really begun. Richard had a messenger dispatched for Mrs. Dorsett and she arrived with a bundle of worn, little baby clothes under her arm. From my window I saw her arrival, riding sideways on a shaggy pony. Her blue calico dress fluttered in the wind. 'Twas a wild, March morning that my baby came to me. Even today the sound of the moaning wind brings back to me memory of that incredible suffering.

Hattie Eliza Russell was a big baby, and she tore her way into existance. The angels of life and death wrestled in that little pioneer fort over her life and over mine. It was due to Mrs. Dorsett's skill that I lived to hear the tiny, pleading wail of my first baby. Strange it was but at the sound of that wail, a half-smothered cry, a great revulsion passed through me. I would have nothing to do with my child. I loathed and hated the thing that had caused me so much cruel suffering. Mrs. Dorsett, with kindly understanding, wrapped up the mite of humanity and took it home with her. So Hattie Eliza took her first horseback ride the day she was born. Contented, I turned on my side and fell asleep. When I awoke it was quite dark. I heard the measured footsteps of the sentry pacing up and down outside the hospital. I thought of the tumble weeds which were rolling out on the dark prairie between me and Hattie Eliza. Mother-love flared into being. I wanted my baby. When morning came Richard went for her. I will never forget the strength in her baby fingers as she wound them around my forefinger. I wondered if she knew how I had felt about her. Compunction overtook me.

Just outside the confines of Fort Bascom stood a store building. It was called "The Settlers' Store" and was operated by a man named Charlie Hopkins. I had known Charlie well in Santa Fé. His sister and I had gone to the Academy together. Her name was Hattie and it was for mother and Hattie Hopkins that I named my first baby.

Charlie Hopkins' wife was a dark, silent girl, the daughter of C.H. Moore, one of New Mexico's early settlers. Mrs. Hopkins' first husband had been killed by the Indians. It seemed that they lived at first with her father, C.H. Moore. Then they took up a place of their own farther down on the Red River. While they were still living with Mr. Moore the young husband would go to his own place each morning to erect the building and get it ready for his wife. One morning he left saying he would be back by noontime. When he failed to return his wife saddled her horse and went in search of him. She found a band of Indians at the new place. On the well-curb lay her husband's lifeless body. Beside herself with grief she ran to where he lay. One of the Indians

111

seized her by the hair and pressed the edge of a knife to her throat. However a renegade Mexican, who had joined the Indian band, interceded for her. Angry, the murderous Indian lifted the young wife bodily and threw her into the well. Fortunately the well was not very deep, neither was there much water in it. However the fall had hurt her, and she had difficulty in dragging herself to the stone curbing above water level. Hours passed and darkness came. She could not get out, and all the time she thought of her husband's lifeless body on the well curb above her. Next morning the renegade Mexican came and helped her out.

One day the soldiers brought to Fort Bascom two Mexican women they had found held prisoners by the Indians. One of them was a middle-aged woman. She had been held captive by the Comanches for so many years her sole language was a Comanche grunt. The other woman was scarcely more than a girl and rather good-looking. Just how they made their escape from the Indian tribe, I no longer remember; but the soldiers had found them along the trail and had brought them to the fort. They were very dirty and covered with vermin. The younger woman spoke Spanish fluently. She told us they had been delayed because the older woman had given birth to a baby. The little papoose had died aborning, and the young woman told us how they had buried it under some bushes and hurried onward. Their pitiful plight aroused the pity of the entire fort. Everyone wanted to do something for them. The two Mexican women were given to the Doctor's wife. The younger woman was so glad to be clean once more. She helped the doctor's wife and was cheerful. Not so the older woman. She had been with the Comanches too long. At last, in desperation the doctor's wife turned her over to the Mexican laundress. I do not remember what became of her, but the younger woman was sent on to Santa Fé.

The soldiers stationed at Fort Bascom received $11.00 per month, plus rations. They were each allowed four pounds of coffee and one-fourth of a pound of tea each month. A bit of salt side was allowed them, and they could have all the hard tack, beans and beef that they wanted. Soap was doled out sparingly. We used a great deal of dessicated potatoes, which looked a great deal like brown sugar. A cup of boiling water poured over a cup of the dessicated potatoes made a stiff-dough that could be shaped into cakes and fried. It was not very good.

In our living room there was a fireplace which in summer never had a fire in it. The current of air passing up the tall chimney made the hearth of the fireplace the coolest place in the house. Inside the fireplace I placed newspapers and there I placed my pans of milk. On the hearth I placed Hattie Eliza's little cradle. One day I heard the newspapers inside the fireplace rattling, and there I found two large rattlesnakes. They had come for a drink from the milk pan. When I thought how easily they might have crawled into the cradle with my baby, I was not able to sleep that night.

As the hot summer wore on Hattie Eliza grew peevish and I spent most of my time bending over her cradle. She had grown to be a pretty child with the large dark eyes of my mother. The new-born look had left her small face and her round, little head was covered with ringlets. One August morning I thought she was sleeping too long. I went and lifted her from her cradle. It was a long, long time before I could realize that I held in my arms a little, dead baby. I stood and held her, saying nothing until Richard came and took her from me.

After that, life was horribly empty at Fort Bascom. Day succeeded day and I found no joy in the common tasks that awaited me. Richard watched me with pity, and at last asked for a leave of absence that he might take me to Santa Fé. It had been months since I had been outside the fort and in spite of myself I enjoyed the long horseback ride to Santa Fé.

When I visited the hospital in Santa Fé, I found Mrs. Sutton grown helpless and senile; yet she knew me and called me "Sis," and asked about mother and Will. Mrs.

George Hebert was there with her first baby. It was a comfort to me to hold the baby in my empty aching arms.

When our leave of absence was over I found a new side-saddle on my dappled gray. It was Richard's gift to me, and he could not have given me anything I would have appreciated more.

We did not stay much longer in Fort Bascom for Richard was ordered to report to Fort Union for further orders. I think of Fort Bascom tenderly, for a little grave is there where Hattie Eliza is sleeping.

CHAPTER SEVEN

Tecolote Traders 1866-1871

WE NOW waited in Fort Union for Richard to be mustered out of the army. The Civil War was over and Richard had begun to long for civilian life. The government wanted to send him to Fort Garland in Colorado Territory, where he would have been in command, but Richard refused. He and Mr. DeHague had planned a new business venture.

I remember that while we waited in Fort Union for Richard to be mustered out, a company of soldiers was sent to Trinidad, Colorado, under the command of Colonel Alexander. Atrocities had been committed there under the leadership of Ka-ni-ha-che.

Ka-ni-ha-che was a celebrated chief of the Moache Utes, attached at this time to the Cimarron Agency in northeastern New Mexico. His band roamed the Stonewall and Cucharas valleys in Colorado until the early seventies, when they were removed to the Los Pinos Agency in western Colorado.

Colonel Alexander was a new man, fresh from the east. When he reached Trinidad, he held a parley with the Indians. He did not know what Colonel Carson might have told him. Politeness and kindness only make the Indians feel that you are afraid of them. They promised Colonel Alexander, with their tongues in their cheeks, that they would be good and never make their white brothers any trouble. When Colonel Alexander withdrew his troops the Indians once more fell on the little village of Trinidad.

Colonel Alexander returned. This time there was no parley. He overtook Ka-ni-ha-che and his warriors at Long's Canyon on the old George Thompson ranch. The Long's Canyon fight was a decisive one. It finished the Utes in that section of the country, although old Ka-ni-ha-che escaped with his life.

I remember my last Fourth of July at Fort Union. Some of the soldiers had free whiskey given them. One that had been assigned us as cook became intoxicated and wandered away. I went ahead with the cooking for I knew what Independence Day meant to the soldiers. Louis was a good boy and Independence Day came but once a year. However, that evening a drunken private came to our quarters where I was alone. He ordered me in a loud insulting voice to prepare supper for him. An officer who happened to be passing heard his loud voice. He came in and broke his cane over the drunken private's back. That private was sentenced to thirty days of the California Walk. I tried hard to harden my heart against him, but I was glad when he was mustered out of the army before his punishment ended.

At last there came a day when we left Fort Union forever; Fort Union that had sheltered and protected me since I was seven. I tried not to look back, for a new life was beginning for me, and it is better to walk with our eyes before us than with them cast behind.

As the western country cleared of Indians, emigrants began pouring in. Las Vegas began to grow and other settlements sprang up near the forts. The freighting of military supplies from the Missouri River to points other than the forts required the services of hundreds of oxen and mule teams. Hundreds of freighters did a big business. Las Vegas soon out-stripped Santa Fé as a business center.

The beautiful, fertile valleys surrounding Fort Union were soon under cultivation. A ready market at high prices was found at Fort Union for all the grain and forage that could be produced. The land of enchantment began to prosper amazingly. Many of the officers at Fort Union, including numerous members of the medical staff and private soldiers, homesteaded in those valleys. Fort Union was closed and abandoned in February of 1891. Yet the country was constantly receiving infusions of new blood.

Richard and Mr. DeHague decided in 1866 to go to Tecolote, New Mexico and to establish a trading post there. Tecolote was simply a watering place west of Las Vegas on the Santa Fé Trail. George Moore and David Winternitz had already established a $75,000 freight outfit there. Tecolote, like all New Mexico towns, was just a collection of low adobe houses and narrow crooked streets. It was thriving and prosperous and we felt we would do well there.

Tecolote—the Indian name means "owl"—had a romantic and mysterious origin. Old mine shafts, crumbling and long unused were there. There were old ovens, hunks of slag and bits of half-melted ore. Even the oldest Mexican inhabitant could not recall ever having heard his grandfather tell the story of the old mines.

We bought a site for our trading post in 1866, and immediately erected the great stone building that was to be both store and dwelling. The store was wide and spacious. Its low ceiling was crossed by massive beams. The long shelves were piled high with everything under the sun. There were implements, feed, food, household furnishings, clothing, saddles, bridles, harness and Navajo blankets. There were strings of red peppers and jars of *azule* or Indian corn. There were jars of Mexican beans and piles of golden pumpkins.

We bought everything the Mexicans or Indians had for sale or trade. Early each morning they would come wandering in from the red, rolling hills. Some would come on foot driving before them a goat or a sheep. Some would come in carts or wagons bringing cheese, peppers, a coop of red chickens or a sack of white Spanish onions. Some would come in leading burros loaded down with firewood. Both the Indians and the Mexicans raised corn and we bought it from them for 8c a pound. A hind quarter of mutton or goat meat could be had for about 50c.

Our records show that in the month of October, when we opened our little trading post, we bought of C.H. Moore at Fort Union a bill of goods amounting to $3,257. This amount was more than duplicated each month thereafter. We also bought great bills of goods from C.H. Kitchen at Las Vegas and we bought out the entire stock of E.M. Murphy in Tecolote. Everything was high. 25% was claimed by the wholesalers and $10.00 a hundred weight was added for freight. As most things were hauled from Leavenworth this freight rate was not exorbitant.

We bought pottery, blankets and beadwork from the Mexicans and Indians, and we were usually able to trade these things to wagoners eastward bound. We traded corn for Indian blankets and turquoise and silver jewelry. When we traded corn for an Indian blanket, two Indians would hold the blanket by its four corners. The amount of shelled corn the blanket would hold bought the blanket. We used old Mexican measures for everything. Our corn measure we called a "fanega." It was made from a buffalo hide. The purchaser held the hide and was permitted to shake it down three times. The amount of shelled corn the old hide measure would hold was about two and one-half bushels. Our yard measure was the Spanish "vara"—thirty-three and a third inches in length.

Our trading post at Tecolote was a meeting place for all the nomads of that desert land: Indian men wrapped in gaudy blankets, Mexican women in black-fringed shawls; cowboys in red shirts and big hats; brown babies in nothing at all, sat, leaned, stood and squatted all over the place.

It was very exciting when the freight trains pulled in. Then the nomads gathered from far and near, and the bartering would go on for days. Once I bartered two cows and a bull for material enough to make me two dresses. One was of heavy moire silk—blue and black water weave. The other was a lavender and black silk brocade. The two patterns cost me the equivalent of $125.00. The material was good. Daughters, then unborn, had to help me wear out those two dresses.

Richard always wanted me to look well, so I dressed as well and as becomingly as I could. I never permitted myself to wear a soiled dress or apron. I never went with my hair uncombed. Each afternoon I bathed and dressed clean and fresh. Personal cleanliness has ever been one of life's necessities for me. Mexican labor was cheap and I always had a woman to help me. It was often hard to teach them how to cook and they always broke my best dishes.

We had five living rooms behind the store. They were cool and pleasant. The thick stone walls resisted both heat and cold. The windows were long and narrow running from ceiling to floor. I draped them with a gay silken print. The floor I had covered with Navajo rugs, which I never really wanted. I remember how I longed for a flowered Brussels carpet. The beds were four-posters. Richard made them for me on his new turning lathe. I was so proud of those four-posters, and kept the spreads and the valances white as snow. Pictures in great, gilt frames I hung on my walls. A lamp with a red shade sat on the claw-footed center table. There were the inevitable red geraniums. I had several pieces of red plush furniture brought by wagon train from Leavenworth. Our chairs were split-bottomed. Over the kitchen door on deer antlers was Richard's array of rifles.

In my kitchen was a nice step-stove. It, also, had come from Leavenworth and had cost Richard a pretty penny. That stove was the light of my eyes and the joy of my heart. It was made like two stair-steps. Each step was used for cooking. The oven heated nicely and many a savory roast did I bake in it. That stove was the envy of all my neighbors. One woman offered me $50 for it.

'Most everyone in Tecolote baked in outdoor, bee-hive ovens.

There were many Penitentes among the Mexicans in Tecolote. They were fanatically religious persons.[35] At Easter they would make crude whips of the knife-like blades of the soap weed and would flog themselves until their poor backs were bloody. They had other strange rituals. I have seen them carrying small images or statues over their fields of corn, praying that the field would yield more bountifully.

It was in Tecolote that an old Spaniard gave a little Indian slave boy to Richard. The Mexicans often captured and made slaves of the Navajo Indians. Indeed, they were encouraged by the government to do so. General Sibley is reported to have recommended: "It is a wise thing to encourage private enterprise against both the Navajo and the Apache Indians, and the enslaving of them."

Our "José Russ" as the Mexicans called him was a problem child. Ambitious and willing, his little feet were forever running errands for me. Yet the truth was not in him. The wild tales that he told of ghosts and goblins scared the little Mexicans silly. Watch out, he said, for the Tecolote Spirit. "The Tecolote wanders around like a bat. When the Tecolote looks at you you are powerless. There is nothing you can do. He never hurts an Indian, for the Tecolote is an Indian, but he has no use for a Mexican. He has been known to string Mexicans up by their heels in a cottonwood tree. He has been known to bore a hole in the top of their heads while they hung there. Then their brains drip out slowly, slowly. The Tecolote hates Mexicans. Whenever the Tecolote looks at a Mexican, that Mexican's liver will begin to melt. There is nothing anyone can do to save himself."

José Russ was a liar. He was also a thief. Nothing was safe from his pilfering fingers. Candy, colored soap and candles disappeared from the store whenever he went there. Finally, there came a day when Richard had to deliver a load of corn to the Navajo reservation. I sim-

120

ply insisted that he take José with him. When Richard came back he told me that almost the first Navajo they met had been José's father. Great was the old Indian's joy at the return of his son. I was glad to get rid of the first and only slave I had ever had.

DeHague was Indian Agent and Richard had a commission to deliver corn and salt to the tribesmen. Corn we bought cheaply from the Mexicans and traded to the Indians for cattle. Our records show that we traded corn at Fort Defiance, Las Vegas and Fort Union.

Near Tecolote was a salt-sink and Richard would go there with freight wagons and a number of Mexican laborers for salt. The barefooted Mexicans would wade out into the sink and shovel the salt up into windrows. The waves lapping over the windrows would clean it nicely. Then it was loaded into the wagons and hauled away. A cleaner, whiter grade of salt might be procured at another sink farther down in Texas, but the Indians had been so hostile there the government had forbidden the men going there.

In 1869 Mr. DeHague was appointed Forage Agent at Tecolote and we made some money furnishing feed to the freight teams. Every extra penny we could lay hands on we spent buying Texas long-horns. The entire profit of the post was so invested. Richard had never forgotten his dream of being a cattle rancher.

In May of 1867 little Katie Elmira came to us. Another cradle swayed on the hearth rug and I now sang as I worked, the grave at Fort Bascom was only a sad memory.

One of the few white men in Tecolote was a young German by the name of George Storz. He ran a little commissary there and was married to a pretty Mexican girl. She was a half-sister to the Mrs. Charlie Hopkins I had known at Fort Bascom. I mention the George Storz family here not only because they were our friends and neighbors in Tecolote, but because they followed us to the Stonewall country in Colorado. The lives of the Storz and the Russell families quietly flowered on together.

In the second year of our stay in Tecolote news reached us of the death of Colonel Kit Carson.[36] Strange that death should always seem so unreal. I have never been able to think of Colonel Carson as dead. Kit Carson, the Happy Warrior, gone to his rest? Along the old Santa Fé Trail there are stone walls his hands had built. In the forest are chips left by his axe. I never think of Colonel Carson as a bundle of dust in Taos cemetery. He is hawk wings against a western sky; a living soul launched out upon a sea of light.

In the fall of 1869 another child was born to Richard and me. It was fun to watch Katie Elmira fold her dimpled hands behind her and stand watching the interloper in her small cradle.

Richard now began thinking of selling the post and hunting a ranch were we might drive our herd of cattle. In January of 1870, however, his brother, John, came to us from Chicago. John was ill with tuberculosis and we laid our own plans aside that we might give him the care that he needed. The clean, warm air of New Mexico healed him as it had so many before him, and, in June of that year, he and Richard began planning a pack-horse to Cheyenne, Wyoming. I was appalled when they told me, for Cheyenne lay many miles northward. John was not only still weak and ailing, but he was a tenderfoot. He had scarcely been on a horse in his life. The Indians along the trail to Cheyenne were still hostile and war-like. However, the new Union Pacific railroad had just reached Cheyenne, Wyoming. John and Richard were determined they would go to Cheyenne, looking as they went for a new ranch location, and when they reached Cheyenne they would sell their pack animals and go back to Chicago on that new Union Pacific train. By this time Mr. DeHague had absconded with much of our money and Richard was beginning to be discouraged.

Long days of waiting followed Richard's and John's departure. At last I had a letter postmarked from Manitou, Colorado. I still have the letter he wrote me. On one side he drew a clumsy picture of himself drinking a glass of Manitou water and, inscribed it, "To Katie Elmira's very good health." He wrote that for John's sake, they were resting at Manitou House, although John had stood the trip well. He wrote that the proprietor had offered to sell them Manitou House for $240.00! He spoke of the fun they had had on the trip, and how John's appetite had come back, color had come to his face and strength to his limbs.

They reached Cheyenne, Wyoming, in good time, and bought tickets on the first train to leave Cheyenne going eastward. Everyone turned out to see the departure. Being unfamiliar with locomotives, Richard and John chose a seat in the center of the coach so as to be equidistant from either end. The big locomotive breathing smoke and fire was brought from its lair in the round house. It backed up and was hooked onto the day coach. Then began the long trip across the prairies. The Indians east of Cheyenne had heard about the big iron monster. Now they heard its frightful roar. They saw the great beast with red flaming eyes bearing down upon them. They saw the black beast lay back its ears and start running. Nothing in all the Indians annals could equal it. They were frightened but undaunted. All the night before their war drums had sounded, now they were ready and waiting. Sometimes I like to think about the sound of their war drums, the cry of a lost race calling.

When the engineer got full steam ahead and was gathering speed he saw twenty Indian warriors drawn up square across the track. He ordered "full-steam-ahead" and roared right into that bunch of warriors at the incredible speed of twenty-five miles an hour. Arrows began flying through the open windows. John and Richard took refuge under the seats in the coach. At the first stop much blood was found on the cow-catcher.

Richard visited awhile with his relatives in Chicago. They tried hard to get him to go into the mercantile business there. He had not been in Chicago long, however, until he knew definitely that he would never be

123

happy anywhere but in the West. It was over his sister's tearful protests that he returned to New Mexico. He came home by way of the Overland Stage. New Mexico had no railroad. Traveling by stage, Richard said, was a most wholesome social experience, for nowhere else does one meet so many agreeable people.

He had been gone altogether about three months, the longest period of time we had ever been separated. He returned a bit unexpectedly. Even at that I was watching for him at the kitchen window. It seemed to me I had stood at that window ever since he and John had faded out of sight with their pack horses. Now I saw the Overland Stage swing into sight around the bend in the red dirt road. The four horses were loping easily, the canopied stage swaying. A moment later he was standing in front of the trading post surrounded by Indians and loafers. His eyes were on mine as I stood by the window. I heard his laughing voice. I heard him open the door and cross the floor to come and stand beside me. I simply stood there transfixed with joy. I could not move nor could I speak to him. Neither did Richard speak. He simply took me in his arms and held me while the troubled world rolled onward and left us.

Looking back on my life at Tecolote I find that the big things seem little and the little things seem big. Someway I have managed to push the grief DeHague's dishonesty caused us into the back of my mind, until at last it is only a shadow. But the dog the swindler left behind him I remember with joy.

Someone had found the dog when it was but a puppy whimpering along the Santa Fé Trail. He brought him to the trading post and gave him to DeHague. We called him *Parejo*, which is a Spanish word meaning "even." This was because DeHague had the puppy's ears trimmed off even. Parejo was the best watch dog we ever had, but as he grew older he became ferocious. He taught my children their first toddling steps. With their little hands clutched in his long hair he walked slowly beside them. Finally we kept him chained for he was so large and ferocious he could easily have killed a man. One morning as I stood dressing, I heard someone knocking at the back door. In the same moment I heard Parejo's chain dragging across the kitchen floor. Half-dressed, I ran calling out to the person to go quickly away or the dog would kill him. Parejo charged past me and I clutched at his collar. He dragged me with him as if I were a doll. A Mexican was standing on the back steps. Parejo sank his yellow fangs deep into the man's calf. Our united screams brought Richard from the store. We had trouble prying Parejo loose. After that we kept Parejo more closely chained and when we moved to Stonewall we took him with us, and there he saved my life.

Richard sold part of his cattle and managed to pay all outstanding debts. Then one morning when things were beginning to look more hopeful, 10,000 pounds of shelled corn in the storage room caught fire from spontaneous combustion. We tried to save it, but when the fire was extinguished, great piles of blackened corn smoldered behind the trading post for weeks. Richard bought eighty head of hogs and fattened them on the damaged corn. Then he hauled them to Fort Sumner, and sold them to Lucien Maxwell,[37] receiving $1,000 for them. I remember how he handed me that money saying, "Marian, you are the only partner I shall ever again have."

In the fall of 1871 Richard sold the trading post and we made preparations to leave Tecolote. Our half-formed plan was to locate in the San Luis Valley in Colorado. Richard had sent herds of cattle there to fatten, and he knew that it was rich and fertile. We hoped to file on 160 acres under the Homestead Act. We knew that both grass and water were plentiful in the San Luis Valley and Richard knew of a little creek where our cattle would stay fat and sleek through the long winters.

We decided to take on the first trip one freight wagon and team, and two saddle horses. After we located, Mr. Russell would send for the rest of things. The George Storz family were planning to follow us wherever we might settle. So we left Tecolote in September; left to seek those green fields that always lie at the far away end of the rainbow.

Richard had insisted that I take the two children and go by stage to Uncle Dick Wootten's tollgate on the Raton Pass.[38] He thought it would not tire me so much as riding in the heavily loaded freight wagon. I was to wait a few days before starting. The morning he finished packing and stood by the wagon saying Good-Bye, Katie Elmira, our little sun-bonnet baby, came and insisted that she was going with him. I can see her yet, standing there in the bright, morning sunshine tying her sun-bonnet under her dimpled chin. When I shook my head at her she looked at me with round, reproachful eyes. "Daddy cannot go alone. I won't let him," she stated. They drove away together, her little sunbonnet bobbing up and down at his elbow. 'Tis the little things of life I remember so well.

As I turned back into my dismantled home a great nostalgic longing took hold of me. It was as if, for a moment, I was permitted a glimpse into the future, and knew how my heart would stay ever in the arid hills of New Mexico. Often I have heard old-timers laughing about the heat and the dust of the desert. I have heard them say jokingly that Hell would seem cool after living in Santa Fé. I had heard them say that the burning sands of the desert had sucked old-timers so dry that they could not pray. I had laughed with them; but now I was leaving my desert for the green hills far away. I was leaving the land I had come to as a child sitting on the high spring seat of a covered wagon; sitting there by my mother. I was soon to learn that all the fair, green reaches of the whole wide earth could never be as dear to me as the tortured beauty of my desert.

It was with sorrow in my heart that I climbed one morning aboard the Overland Stage. My baby's head lay heavy on my arm. My heart was heavy within me. I left the land of the tinted hills, where lakes of purple haze filled the shallow, arid basins. Here among these

126

red hills, I had watched the hump-backed bison give place to the Texas long-horn. Here I had come to see the pinto pony take the place of the burro and the wild mustang. I left the land I loved with its ranches, convents, churches, priests, bandits and gamblers. I left the land of enchantment.

I shall never forget that stage ride across the wastes. Once we came to a place where the carcasses of so many dead mules lay by the roadside that I was led to ask about them. The driver explained that the previous spring a strange epidemic attacked mules and burros all over the West. The place we had just passed was where a mule-driven freight train had been left stranded; every mule in the wagon train had died there.

As we drew near Uncle Dick Wootten's toll gate I began to think of Richard and Katie, my sun-bonnet baby. My heart reproached me for disloyalty, reproached me for looking backward so sadly. When I climbed down from the stage, I stood looking for the freight wagon. Surely it camped near the toll gate. Then I heard Katie Elmira's piping voice. She had been sent up the trail to meet me. She held out her wee arms for the baby. Richard was camped beyond the bend in the trail. All day she had kept watch for me.

At Trinidad, in Colorado, we drove our freight wagon under some tall cottonwoods and made camp for the night. A red bridge spanned the shining river we had forded so long ago. Next morning we ran into an old friend on the street—a man we had known in Santa Fé. He was Judge William Bransford, close associate of Kit Carson and Lucien Maxwell.[39] He was Justice of the Peace in little Trinidad. He had been a wagon master in the old days, hauling supplies from Kansas City to the stores of Bent and St. Vrain both at Taos and Santa Fé.[40]

Judge Bransford followed us to our camp that September evening and we talked long of the old days. We talked of Colonel Carson, Carlos Beaubien, Guadalupe Miranda, Lucien Maxwell, General Kearny and Charles Bent.[41] It was nice to meet an old friend so unexpectedly, just as we were planning to leave old friends behind us. He tried that evening to get Richard to go no farther, but to stay and start a store in Trinidad. But by this time Richard was determined to become a cattle rancher; the dream of his life was to be a dream no longer.

We broke camp early next morning and were two miles out on the north road when the sun came up. We halted then at a little house by the roadside to inquire the road to the San Luis Valley. The friendly little woman who answered my husband's inquiry by directing us onward, tried to discourage us at the same time. She told us she and her husband had just moved away from the San Luis Valley. They had not enjoyed living there, she said. She did not think we would find it at all pleasant. She talked of cold winters, isolation and bad roads.

I have often wondered since what our lives would have been had we not stopped that morning to inquire about the road that lay ahead. The destiny that rules our lives seems to love to manifest itself in trivial things. Had we gone on into the San Luis Valley, would we have been happy? Had we not stopped at that house by the wayside would Richard have been spared to me? Would he have lived out his life in a normal manner and not have fallen before an assassin's bullet? But destiny came to us in the guise of a friendly little woman in a clean faded gingham who leaned against the wheel of our wagon. "Go to the St. John's Valley," said the woman. "It surely is a second Eden. It lies thirty-eight miles up the River Purgatoire. There you will find feed and water for your cattle. There you will be happy." So it was that Destiny sent us searching for happiness along the River Purgatoire.

But Jordan is a hard road to travel, and evening found us only half way to Eden. Evening found us discouraged. The too-narrow valley we had followed all the way from Trinidad, was rimmed on either side by rocky, barren hills. The Purgatoire wound back and forth across the narrow valley and our heavy wagon lurched and tumbled.

Mid-afternoon on the second day of our travel, we saw the great Stone Wall rising from the blue mists at its feet. Behind it, with all its towers and turrets, rose the white-capped Sangre de Cristo Mountains. The Sangre de Christo, meaning Blood of Christ mountains, we thought were well named, for their snowy tops were stained blood-red by the setting sun.

Gradually, as we climbed, the valley widened until we came out onto a natural meadow interspersed with tall pines. The mighty wall before us grew higher and higher. This strange freak of nature, the great stone wall, runs through the entire states of Colorado and Wyoming, and is one of the wonders of the Rocky Mountain region. Its precipitous walls are as smooth as if made by the hand of man. When we came to the base of the wonder, the road turned and ran parallel with it. Suddenly we came to a gap in the towering wall and drove through a natural gateway. God, it seemed, had decided to let us into the Garden.

We camped that night in the loveliest spot I had ever seen. A small natural meadow between the great wall and the tall Sangre de Cristos. We unrolled our camp bed on the fragrant pine needles and slept that night under the stars. How well do I remember how the moon and the river sang together. It was witchery to lie under the star-spangled sky and to hear the little mountain river go singing by on its way to the ocean. I heard our hobbled horses grazing. I heard my sun-bonnet baby murmur in her sleep in the wagon. The cold, wet dew fell on my face and on the heavy mass of my hair. I tried as I lay there to let this new, strange beauty of the earth sink into my soul. I did not know then that the moon I saw rise above the dark stone wall, would rise always behind that same wall. I would know no more moonlight on the desert.

The morning was startlingly cold and the children and I huddled over the breakfast fire Richard built for us. How prodigal he was of the wood! After the cooking was over we laid log after log on the fire. When the day grew warmer we went house hunting, or at least looked for a place to build our cabin. We found a level place by a clear, cold spring. Water meant so much to us. "Here is the place," said Richard, "here is where we will build our new home."

Richard renamed the valley that morning, "Stonewall Valley." Stonewall Valley it has been called ever since. The soil was rich and fertile, the grass thick and abundant. There were deer and fish to be had for the taking. Wild plum and choke cherries grew along the little river. There was a high range of mountains to protect us from the cold winds of winter.

I like to remember Richard as he was that morning, the light of new dreams in his eyes. I like to remember how he walked barehead under the pines. A new domain he planned for us that morning, a domain to be built by his own hands. Some times I have wondered why, when one asks so little of life, that little is so often denied—just a little moon, a little silver spoon, a little copper kettle. We had mountain trout for breakfast and while we ate them two deer came down from the timbered slope and watched us.

We were not the first settlers in Stonewall. There was a white trapper living in a tiny cabin there. His name was J. A. Weston whose son runs our local blacksmith shop there today. It was in his honor that the town of Weston was named. Murdo McKenzie, in later years, tore down Weston's cabin and built his nice summer home there.[42] Mr. McKenzie said he had searched the world over for the ideal place for a summer cottage. He found that place in Stonewall Valley.

The next morning we returned to Trinidad for supplies. It was downhill all the way and the horses stepped out blithely. Richard sent word back to Tecolote for a man to come and help him, a young fellow by name John Sanger. John was one of our family in Stonewall for many years thereafter.

130

CHAPTER EIGHT

Stonewall Valley Ranch
1871-1936

THE YEARS that followed were busy ones; sometimes it seemed that more tasks were allotted me than my busy hands could ever do. Somehow I found time to write to mother, who had gone again to Kansas City, and to brother Will. I tried hard not to let mother know how much I missed her, but she read between the lines and knew she was needed. She arrived one November morning. She said she had heard that the Ute Indians were thick in the Stonewall Valley, and she was wondering if Richard would leave me alone often. She pictured me sitting half-frightened in our covered wagon waiting for Richard. So she arose one morning, packed her horsehair trunk, and hit the trail westward. Dear Mother!

While Richard and John cut logs for the house I busied myself around camp. I could hear the sound of their axes not far away in the timber. As soon as a part of the house was laid up, we moved in, for winter was coming; the morning and evenings were cold and frosty. We had no partitions, no doors, no windows. We hung a heavy Indian blanket in the doorway and chained Parejo there for protection. Our new home was on the Ute Trail to the Cimarron Agency and we often saw the Indians passing.

One morning, before mother arrived, I was at work when I chanced to glance out the open window, and there was a tall Ute warrior coming up the pathway from the spring. Paralyzed with fright I crawled under the bed, taking both children with me. Scarcely were we tucked out of sight when Parejo gave his man-growl. Katie Elmira was frightened and kept as silent as a mouse, but the baby cooed and murmured. Above the barking of the dog and the frantic beating of my own heart, I heard the Indian's low grunt of chagrin when he found his entrance barred by Parejo. There came then the sound of moccasined feet following the outer wall of the house around to the open window. I thought of Katie Elmira's curly locks decorating that red heathens belt, and I prayed as I had never prayed before.

The Ute's grotesquely-painted face and blanket-draped shoulders appeared at the open window. His beady eyes searched the room. Would it be safe, he seemed to be wondering, to enter? My baby, just learning to talk, said, "Whose dat Mama," and the evil black eyes found us where we crouched in the shadows. The blanket slipped from his shoulders as he heaved himself up and through the window; but he reckoned without Parejo. The dog could not quite reach the window, but he projected himself with fury between me and that horror-filled window. He stood at the end of his chain; stood up on his hind feet and with slavering jaws dared the intruder to enter. I prayed that the chain would break and those fangs would sink in the flesh of the Indian. The big Ute, then almost through the window, halted. He looked the big dog in the eyes for a moment. Parejo growled like thunder. The hair on his back bristled. Slowly the dark hands let go of the window sill, and the greasy black hair parted above the black beady eyes disappeared from the window. I heard moccasined feet leaving. Parejo still growled and tugged at his chain as we crawled from under the bed.

After the first two rooms were finished and the roof on, I began plastering the inner walls as I had seen the Mexican women do in Santa Fé. It was long, tedious work. My hands became rough and reddened; but I did not stop until all the rough log walls were plastered.

Richard, then, made a door from boards he had hewn with an axe. We had no glass in the windows until we were able to go once more to Trinidad. The weather was getting bitterly cold, so I wrung flour sacks out in deer tallow and stretched them tightly over the open casings.

We had mother's candle moulds, and when Richard killed a deer I moulded candles from the tallow. Mother's candle mould would make four candles at once. It was not long until I had my winter's supply of candles laid away. When our things from Tecolote came I had my nice oil lamps, but I still liked my candles. Even today I keep my tallow candle handy, although my daughter's home is lighted with electricity.

I go back in memory to that first winter we spent behind the great Stonewall. There was our new little house smelling of fresh-hewn pine. There was a great pile of wood where I went to bring in heaping baskets of fragrant wood-chips. Fuel in New Mexico had always been so scarce that I reveled in the abundance in Stonewall. When cold December brought the snow, we had shelter, food, warmth and light. There is so little more for which to strive.

When the wind began to blow cold among the trees, the mountain blue birds left our valley, but the noisy, squalling blue jays stayed on to fly like great blue blossom through the whirling snow flakes.

Our home was thirty-five miles from a white neighbor. Simple though it was, and meagerly furnished, and despite the danger near us, we were happy. One is usually proud of the work of one's hands. When I hung framed pictures on the walls I had whitewashed, and put my lace curtains at the windows; when I had put our books on shelves by the great roaring fireplace, then I thought my home not only cozy, but pretty.

Mother had gone to visit Will in California. We were too safe and comfortable now to suit her. She was always a pioneer faring westward!

Richard spent much time in Stonewall Valley hunting and fishing. The winter was long and cold. Before spring arrived we learned an unexplainable fact about weather conditions in Stonewall: It was many degrees warmer below the wall than above it! Our home was above the wall so we planned to change it. Perhaps our years in New Mexico made us feel the cold in Stonewall more keenly. Often on stormy nights we would draw our beds out in front of the fireplace and fall asleep listening to the crackle of the flames and the whispering fall of the snow flakes.

One day in December of that first winter of 1871, when all the little cedar trees and the tall, blue spruces were bending beneath their weight of snow, a covered wagon pulled in through the gap in the wall and came to halt at our cabin. O joy! The George Storz family had come to join us. Bareheaded I ran out through the snow to welcome our neighbors.

The Storz's, taking advantage of our hard-earned knowledge, built their home below the wall. The home that they founded still stands, and George's son lives in it.

Before spring came, Richard bought a relinquishment below the wall and began to build improvements upon it. Soon he built a dam across the end of the valley and in no time at all had a little lake there. Six more children came to Richard and me. Elinor Agusta Russell, born in November of 1872, was the first white child to be born in the Stonewall Valley. Her birth was followed in quick succession by two little boys hardly two years apart, Harold Damewood and Oliver Earl. Then came Marian Ethel and two more little boys. In admitting the fact that I brought nine children into life, it seems that must have been too many. Yet each one was welcome, and looking back upon them they seem life's greatest blessing.

Sixty years is a long time to stay in one place, even in a little apple-green valley. The first years we spent fighting Indians and carving a new home in a wilderness. The first years I spent rocking babies. Richard became storekeeper and postmaster. He established a

134

saw and planing mill. With our $1,000 from the sale of hogs to Lucien Maxwell we had bought cattle and now we drove them to Stonewall from Tecolote. Again the big things seem little, and little things seem big. Among that first herd of cattle was a snow-white cow with a sprinkling of rose-colored freckles. We called her Pacheco. Her snowy descendants still appear in my son's herd of cattle. The last one, called Snow Ball, belongs to my son Harold's wife—she whom I have commissioned to write down these memoirs for me.

We milked as many of the cows as we could, and during the first years made money selling butter. We would send freight wagons with wheat, flour and butter to Fort Lyons, Colorado, and exchange it for buffalo meat and other provisions.[43] We sent butter to Santa Fé and Taos, and exchanged it for chile peppers, white onions and Mexican beans. Once John Sanger took a load of butter to Santa Fé and brought back in exchange several sacks of white onions, two strings of chile and $240.00 in cash.

We churned five times a week and made from thirty-five to forty pounds at a churning. Richard, always clever with his hands, made a butter-table where he could work out the great rolls of butter. He made a barrel churn that would churn a great quantity at one time. We would wrap our rolls of butter in cheese cloth and pack it in salt. Sometimes we sent it as far away as Missouri, where we received 40c a pound for it.

The Utes had a habit of coming to perch on the corral fence at milking time. Always they brought their tin cans and buckets, hoping for a hand out. So many got to coming that one evening Richard refused to fill their cans. They went away sullen and resentful. That night they burned our haystacks—the winter feed for our cattle.

Richard had several unneeded freight wagons and was able to trade them to the Mexicans at Stonewall for wheat. The wheat he sent to Fort Lyon by John Sanger. We expected him back in three weeks, but two months passed and we heard nothing from him. Richard grew fearful. The Cheyennes were on the war path against their old enemies, the Utes. The Utes were always afraid of the Cheyennes. A band of the Utes were camped on the mountain about the Storz ranch during those days. Finally one morning they broke camp and started for Cimarron Agency. They filed past our house in what seemed an endless procession. The more intelligent Cheyennes seemed to know just what the Utes would do—try to reach the protection of the Cimarron Agency. They circled around and met the Utes that morning as they came out on the Cimarron Trail. In the fight that ensued that band of Utes was almost demolished. After the fight, Richard went for John Sanger. Fear had held him at Fort Lyons.

One day when George Irwin was about nine years old, he was riding in Romaine Canyon with one of the Storz boys. A band of Utes saw them and gave chase. They most likely wanted to steal the boys' saddle horses. Had they known how much George loved his horse they would have known they would get it only over my son's small, dead body. The boys dashed through the band of Utes and headed for home. Five Indians gave chase, but the lads reached us before they did. I shall never forget how my heart turned over as I saw the boys break through the timber with the Indians in hot pursuit.

Other white settlers came to settle in our little valley. Soon we had many neighbors and there was talk of a school at Stonewall.

Richard was a planner, a man of vision. He took possession of the land that lay along the old Ute Trail and made a domain of it. Behind the new house he planted an orchard, the fruit of which he was never to eat. Along the western border of his little domain he planted cottonwood trees and box elders, in whose shade he was never to stand. As the trees that he planted drew taller and taller, the house we had built seemed to grow lower and lower. Today it hovers close to the ground like some mother hen protecting her chickens.

136

The first school, started in 1876, had a short three months term. I can still see Katie Elmira and George Irwin stumping across the road to the little log school house. There was a red bow in Katie Elmira's curly hair and George had on copper-toed boots. I stood watching them through a mist of tears. My babys were growing up.

The first death in Stonewall came in 1876. A log fell on a young lad who was helping Richard with the timber. The settlers gathered to discuss a likely site for a cemetery. We choose a place high up above the blue waters of the little lake Richard had made. It was on a level mesa, the wildest and most beautiful place in our valley. Sixty years ago we made the first grave there. Today there are stones bearing the names of all the old settlers; folks who came and lived out their lives in our applegreen valley.

By 1883, Stonewall had quite a cluster of houses. We had a Sunday School, a school house and a church. We had neighborhood sings and a literary society. We had dances, and sometimes I would take my little melodian and play all night for a dance.

Katie Elmira grew to womanhood. Her mass of hair piled high on her head seemed too heavy a weight for her small white neck. She had grave, sweet eyes and childish parted lips. Her white-ruffled Sunday dresses touched the floor. With womanly dignity she helped direct the work of my household. One night she came into our bedroom and told Richard and me of her love for young Daniel Harvey. Katie Elmira, who only yesterday had tied a little bonnet under her chin to go in the freight wagon with her father! She and young Harvey were married that summer.

Not long after Katie's marriage came the news of mother's death in California. Things were changing, and the people I had loved were leaving me. Nothing in this world can last. Eliza St. Clair Sloan was like a beautiful bird of Paradise. She flew best against the wind. Always she kept her brave face to the wind. Always she loved to follow new trails.

137

Then came Will's death, and I saw him lying with candles burning at his head and at his feet. Did they help light his passing? Did they enable him to see God's face plainly? These are still the unanswered questions!

In 1888, we received notice from the Maxwell Land Grant Company to abandon the domain we had so laboriously wrested from the wildness.[44] Twenty four hours the company gave us to get off our land and out of the valley. Twenty four hours were given us to appear at a hearing in Denver, over two hundred miles away. There were no automobiles then, and we were thirty five miles from the railroad.

History's pages are stained with lies about that great land steal. Coat after coat of whitewash was applied trying to cover up the stains of honest blood. Many men were murdered and unhappiness brought to their families through the loss of their homes on the Maxwell Land Grant.

Many accounts of the Maxwell land steal have been written; it is not my task to write another. Although I still wonder how anything so wrong and cruel could have happened, I recount only how it affected my own life. The Maxwell company deputized armed men and sent them into our Stonewall Valley to drive the settlers there from their homes.

In writing a biography the relative value of days and years must be taken into consideration. There are days that count in time and space as years; and years that count but as a single day. From the day they brought Richard home to me, shot by a Maxwell deputy, until that morning five days later when we laid him to rest, there was pressed a full lifetime of suffering.

When the notice of evacuation was received the Stonewall settlers buzzed like angry bees. It was soon necessary for the Maxwell deputies to barricade themselves in the Coe Hotel. Richard, for some reason, became the spokesman for the settlers. He wrote a letter that was published in the Denver Stockman and Farmer. In it he declared that when the government, for

138

whom he had fought through the Civil War, notified him that a mistake had been made and asked him to leave his home, he would do so, but that no armed Maxwell deputy could drive him away. That letter was the voice of one crying in the wilderness. It was a voice that must be silenced.

Richard was shot while carrying a flag of truce and attempting to negotiate with the deputies who barricaded themselves in the Coe Hotel. The five days that he lay suffering lie open on my heart today. To write of them is not to tear open an old wound for the wound has never healed. The hours that I spent by his bedside were long, hideous hours. The ticking of the clock on the wall was a hammer beating out my own life. The children's frightened faces were pictures against a background of grief and despair. The settlers had burned the Coe Hotel and the deputies had crawled away like serpents thru the tall grass and escaped. The smoke from the burning hotel drifted across Richard's dying face as I sat watching. The messenger we had sent for a doctor had been intercepted by the Maxwell minions. Richard died. There was nothing we could do.

Five hundred armed men followed my husband's body to the little cemetery. I stood dry-eyed and heard the "dust to dust" spoken. The angry thoughts and smarting pain are gone, replaced by the growing knowledge that vengence belongs to God. Richard was called away. I have traveled the length of a dark valley, but it seems today that I am standing on a mountain top above that dark valley.

It seemed at first that the bullet that ended Richard's life had surely ended my own; but there were little stockings that needed mending. Little lunch pails to fill. I carried on.

The children's marriages followed each other in quick succession. Of the nine children that were born to me only six are left. I have sixteen grandchildren, twenty-two great grandchildren and four great, great grandchildren. When we meet at family reunions I am puzzled at times for I cannot tell one from another. At our last reunion on the banks of the little lake Richard built, I watched my young descendants swimming. I tried to count them and couldn't. There were black heads, brown heads and red heads bobbing here and there on the water. There were some with fair hair like Richard's. As I sat watching I couldn't help thinking, "Surely all these young amphibians could not have resulted from that old Fort Union marriage."

Our little apple-green valley is rich in the lore of the red man. Our River Road or highway number 12 was once the old Ute trail and nobody knows how old it is. The little wooded knoll, where Duling Lodge now stands, was once called by the Ute Indians, "Moccasin Hill." 'Tis said that an old Indian ,whose name was Noe, disappeared and was never heard from again, but one of his bloodstained moccasins was found on that little raise of ground and so the Indians called it Moccasin Hill.

There is a cool little lake that lies at timber line which is now called Hidden or Lost Lake. The Utes called it, Ghost Lake. I have never found out why, although I have asked every old Mexican in our valley. It lies like a great, green emerald in a Tiffiny setting of snow-clad mountains. In the evening, when darkness is gathering, strange shadows creep out from its fringe of tall pines. Sometimes there comes a sound like the beating of mighty winds . . . little Ghost Lake of the red man.

There is an Indian burial ground near where the Cottage Hotel now stands. When new highway 12 was put through the valley it ran through the old Indian burial ground. Some of the valley Mexicans refused to work on the highway because of the old Ute legend of "Still Face," the Indian maiden who lies sleeping there, a white man's signet ring on her finger, a white man's babe in her arms and an Indian arrow in her heart.

Monument Lake the Indians once called, Love's Lake. It is said that in those days the waters of Love's Lake were the cleanest and purest water in the valley.

The deer and the wild turkey would drink at no other place. The mountain trout grew large there. The Great Spirit came often to walk on the water of little Love Lake. The great harvest moon would lay a path of golden light across the lake for him, and then the Great Spirit, clad in robes of shining white, would come and walk with gentle footsteps across the peaceful water.

Indians no longer infest the Stonewall trails. The deer and the turkey are fast disappearing from the woodland shadows. The old pioneers are only legend now. There are many white stones on our burial hill.

When I was eighty-nine I made a pilgrimage into the land of yesteryear. I traveled the Santa Fé Trail once more, hoping that I might find there one golden moment spilled from the hand of time. They let me go to the ruins of Camp Nickols. A little dent in the grass marked the place of my nice dugout. A field of corn waved over the trail. With my feet I sought and found the wheel-ruts in the grass where the old wagon trains had gone creaking past on the long-long trail—the old, old trail to Sante Fé. Purple thistle flourished where once had waved the buffalo grass.

At Fort Union I found crumbling walls and tottering chimneys. Here and there a tottering adobe wall where once a mighty howitzer had stood. Great rooms stood roofless, their whitewashed walls open to the sky. Wild gourd vines grew inside the officers' quarters. Rabbits scurried before my questing feet. The little guard house alone stood intact, mute witness of the punishment inflicted there. The Stars and Stripes was gone. Among a heap of rubble I found the ruins of the little chapel where I had stood—a demure, little bride in a velvet cape—and heard a preacher say, "That which God hath joined together let no man put asunder." I found the ruins of my little home where Colonel Carson once had stood beneath a hanging lamp. I heard or seemed to hear again his kindly voice, "Little Maid Marian, you cannot go. I promised your mother to take good care of you." The wind moaned among the crumbling ruins and brought with it the sound of marching feet. I saw with eyes that love to look backward, a wagon train coming along the old trail. I saw a child in a blue pinafore. It was little Maid Marian on the seat of an old covered wagon.

Workmen were busy tearing down the old fortification. They tore my heart down with it. Why not let the old walls stand. Around each crumbling wall, each yawning cellar hole, are gathered precious memories of young America.

Santa Fé had grown larger. Roses mingled with red peppers on old adobe walls. The old wooden gateway through which had flowed the commerce of a nation was gone. Central Plaza was so neat and clean I did not recognize it. A woman in red slacks sat under a great umbrella. Once I had seen Captain Aubry sit in that very spot reading a big newspaper. Old houses stared at me like eyes from an empty skull. Old memories drifted about me like dead leaves in an autumn wind. I went to the chapel and knelt at the self-same altar where my little head had bowed in prayer more than eighty years before. Did Father Lamy's tender hand touch my head in blessing? Did Mother Magdalena's soft, black robes rustle by me in the stillness?

So small were the ruins of Tecolote—my "Little Owl" —that it seemed the red hills were trying to bury the little watering place on the Santa Fé Trail. The stone house was in ruins. Fallen rafters lay aslant windows where once red geraniums had bloomed. An old wooden bed, decrepit and broken lay among the fallen rafters. It was a bedstead that had been made on a turning lathe, a bed that had once boasted a valance white as snow.

Nothing was left of Fort Marcy. Even the adobe walls had fallen. It was strange to stand there that evening where I had played more than eighty years before. Was it imagination, or did I hear voices? The half-remembered voices of children. Were they playing "steal-the-dead-man's-bones" or was it the sound of wind sighing down over the mesa?

Strange to look back when you are old and feeble over the trail you knew as a child!

I live now in the little apple-green valley, and I walk there as one walks in a dream. The faces I love, I see only dimly. The voices I love come from afar. I cannot hear them clearly. The grass in our valley is very green. The mountains rear their white heads above it. The trees that Richard planted wave hands of fairy green above me. Yet I had grown tired of tall trees and cool greenness. My heart has returned to the land the old trail ran through, so long ago. Old paths that wind through the malpais beckon to me. I want to feel the desert sun shine hot on my hands, my face and my breast. The inner chamber of my heart is open wide, its pearls of memory just inside. My thoughts move slowly now like motes behind a faded window blind. I stand listening for the sound of wheels that never come; stand waiting for the clasp of arms long crumbled into dust.

Notes

[1]Fort Snelling, first called Fort Anthony, was established in 1819 at the mouth of the Minnesota River—south of present Minneapolis and across the river from St. Paul—by Colonel Henry Leavenworth. LeRoy R. Hafen and Carl C. Rister, *Western America* (Prentice Hall Inc., New York, 1941), 188. A post was established at the old French trading post of Prairie du Chien (Wisconsin) in 1816. Both military posts played colorful roles in the history of the upper Mississippi Valley during the first half of the Nineteenth Century.

[2]Francis Xavier Aubry, born in Quebec in 1824, was one of the best known and most competent of Santa Fé Trail traders and freighters. His explorations and trading expeditions took him from Fort Leavenworth to Santa Fé, west to San Francisco and south to Mexico. In June 1850 he rode from Santa Fé to Independence, a distance of 850 miles, in five days and sixteen hours in order to win a $10,000 wager. He was killed in an argument in Santa Fé in 1854 by Colonel Richard H. Weighman. See also Ralph P. Bieber, *Southwest Historical Series*, VII, 38-62.

[3]The author means Camp Macky. Located six miles west of Fort Dodge, the original post was called Fort Mann. In 1850 it was known as Camp Macky, and in 1851 Fort Atkinson.

[4]This cut-off saved many days and was several hundred miles shorter than the mountain route. Travelling west it cutoff from the main trail at Cimarron Crossing west of Fort Atkinson and Dodge City, on the Arkansas, and cut southwest through what is now the southwestern corner of Kansas, northwest corner of Oklahoma and northeast corner of New Mexico. It continued past Rabbit Ear Mound following a rough and dry route past Gregg's Round Mound, Point of Rocks to the Canadian or Red River. From the river the cutoff turned more southerly striking Wagon Mound and then joining the main trail below Watrous in New Mexico. See end plate maps.

[5]Dried buffalo dung—"chips"—was the universal fuel of the treeless plains.

[6]The Road Runner or Chaparral Bird is familiar to all who have seen the long legged, long tailed and sharp beaked bird travelling at high speeds along Southwestern trails.

[7]Fort Union was established in 1851 and served as the principal supply post for the entire Southwest until the Santa Fé Railroad was completed to Las Vegas in 1879. It played a vital role throughout the later Indian troubles, the Civil War and the era of settlement.

[8]See W. Wyman, "F. X. Aubry: Santa Fé Freighter, Pathfinder and Explorer," *New Mexico Historical Review*, VII, 1-31.

[9]Sumner became commander of the Ninth Military Department and architect of the New Mexico defense system established to defend the small scattered settle-

ments from Indian raiding parties which had been terrorizing the territory for over a century. He was also founder of Fort Union. *Ibid.*, XIV, 95-105; 160; 340; 343.

[10]In speaking of Indian scouts, the author means Americans or Mexicans employed by the Army to act as scouts for expeditions against the raiding Indians.

[11]In addition to the small Fort Marcy garrison, the Army maintained a head-quarter's staff and paymaster's office in Santa Fé for some years. For a time there was also a quartermaster's depot in the capitol.

[12]The author is confused; it was Governor Peréz who was decapitated in August 1837 in the so-called Chimayo Rebellion. Governor Manuel Armijo succeeded him.

[13]Right Reverend Jean Baptiste Lamy, Bishop of Santa Fé, arrived in New Mexico during the early autumn of 1851 and took charge of reorganizing the old diocese.

[14]The editor wonders if the good sisters thought to check with the U. S. Army quartermaster depot two blocks up the street from the cathedral. The army had shipped in wagon loads of building supplies including oak, mahogany, and other hard woods for use in officers' quarters and other army buildings.

[15]"Political prisoner"—an interesting designation, but it was only five years since the Taos rebellion, and anti-American feeling was still very high in the New Mexico mountain communities as well as in the towns. Acts against Americans were almost daily occurences and resulted in stern measures. Incidentally, this building—the Palace of the Governors—was the same one in which Lieut. Zebulon Pike had been held by the Spaniards in 1807!

[16]It is probable that the prisoner was murdered by members of his own under-ground group to prevent his being forced to reveal the names of other members, places of rendevous and intentions. Secret groups were strong and both civil and military officials were forced to maintain constant vigilance.

[17]Fort Marcy was built after the seizure of New Mexico by Kearny, construction beginning on August 23, 1846. The author here is relating incidents in the 'sixties rather than in the first years after her arrival at Santa Fé.

[18]Camp Nichols was a temporary post established to prevent the Commanches and other tribes from attacking the wagon trains. It was located on the Cimarron cut-off of the Santa Fé trail just across the New Mexico line in what is now Okla-homa. For a description and drawing of the camp see *Colorado Magazine*, XI , 179-186. Note correct spelling is with an "h."

[19]Since Carson arrived in Santa Fé from California on December 25, 1853, the meeting between Marian Russell and Kit Carson took place sometime after that date and before he took up his duties in Taos the following Spring. It is probable that Mrs. Russell's memory slipped on the point of "Little Jo". He had married Maria Josefa Jaramillo of Taos in 1843 and while he was in California "Josefita" —the Spanish diminutive for Josefa—spent some time with relatives in Santa Fé. It is possible that young Marian mistook the relationship, for "Little Jo" is an almost exact translation of Carson's affectionate nickname for his wife. It is true, however, that previous to his marriage to Senorita Jaramillo he had been married to two Indian wives. See Edwin Sabin, *Kit Carson Days*. I, 312-313, II, 637.

[20]Lydia Pinkham's famous patent medicine, of course. Even today in parts of the West great faith is held in the "baby in every bottle" idea.

[21]Gold was discovered on Cherry Creek in 1858 and a major strike in 1859 at Gregory Diggings near Central City west of present Denver resulted in a tremen-dous rush to the gold fields. The flood of gold seekers used the Oregon, Santa Fé and the newly opened Smokey Hill trails. For an excellent eye-witness account see William Hawkins Hedges, *Pike's Peak or . . . Busted!* The Branding Iron Press, Evanston, Ill., 1954.

[22]*jacal*, usually a brush shelter built to protect against wind, storm or sun; in the

146

Southwest these were sometimes more permanently built of adobe, logs or both.

23Probably the great salt beds in the Estancia Valley which had been used for centuries by the Indians, Spaniards and Mexicans. Salt was a highly prized trade commodity from early colonial days. See *New Mexico*, American Guide Series (University of New Mexico Press, Albuquerque, 1945), 294.

24*mañana*, Spanish for "tomorrow". New Mexico has long been known as "The Land of Tomorrow" because of the old canard that when asked to do something the native New Mexican supposedly would reply, "yes, tomorrow"—meaning he wouldn't work today. Actually the New Mexican works hard and well, but he works to live rather than living to work. To those who love the state, its traditions, and its distinctive culture, the phrase means "a land of calm and contentment where time works for man and is not his master."

25This was the first Masonic lodge in New Mexico. Since most of its army officer founders belonged to the Grand Lodge of Missouri, the Fort Union lodge was chartered and administered from that grand lodge. Many famous officers and frontiersman belonged to the Fort Union lodge including Kit Carson.

26Texas longhorn cattle were driven to California during the gold rush era when there was an almost insatiable demand for fresh meat. Garnet M. and Herbert O. Brayer, *American Cattle Trails 1540-1900* (Denver, Colo. 1952), 38*ff.*

27This was General James H. Carleton.

28Carson served brilliantly under most trying circumstances as colonel of the New Mexico Volunteers. He was later breveted a Brigadier General. He was in command of the fort for only a short period in 1864-65.

29Of course, this was not literally true. The Mexican wash women as well as wives of some of the men were "white" although the Americans recognized only those who came from the states as being so. It was a popular assumption with derogatory overtones.

30The abduction and murder of Mrs. White is a well documented New Mexican incident. The White family had been traveling in a train conducted by Captain Francis X. Aubry. White, an experienced Santa Fé trader had left the main train to hurry ahead with a small party. The Indians fell upon the group, killed all the men, destroyed the goods and seized Mrs. White, her young daughter and a negro woman servant. Twelve days later Mrs. White was ruthlessly murdered when a rescue party from Taos, lead by Major William N. Grier, came upon the Indian encampment. The child and the servant were never recovered.

31See Albert W. Thompson, "The Death and The Last Will of Kit Carson," *The Colorado Magazine*, V, No. 5, October 1928, 183*ff.*

32See Laura C. Manson White, "Albert H. Pfeiffer", *ibid.*, X, No. 6, Nov. 1933, 217.

33Mrs. Russell could ride "western style," but the major taught her "proper" riding methods.

34*loco:* the Spanish and Mexican word for crazy. Horses, cattle, sheep, and even goats get the malady from eating certain poisonous plants which grow in some profusion in parts of the plains and the mountains. Frequently affected animals have to be destroyed.

35For an excellent description of the Penetentes see Barron B. Beshoar, "Western Trails to Calvary" *1949 Brand Book* (Denver Posse; Denver, Colo., 1950), 119*ff.*

36See footnote 31 above.

37For an excellent summary of Maxwell's life and adventures see Harold H. Dunham, "Lucien B. Maxwell: Frontiersman and Businessman," *1949 Brand Book* (Denver Posse; Denver, Colo., 1950), 269*ff.*

[38]Wootton's spectacular career was the subject of a noted biography by Howard Louis Conard, *"Uncle Dick" Wootton*, Chicago: W. E. Dibble & Co. 1890. Unfortunately the book, like its subject, must be used with great care.

[39]Judge Bransford had a colorful history. From 1844 to 1847 he was manager of the St. Vrain and Bent livestock operation on the Vigil and St. Vrain land grant in the Arkansas Valley. He worked closely with the Bents and later with the political ring that sought to get control of large Mexican land grants.

[40]The Bents and St. Vrains formed one of the largest and most successful of the Santa Fé trail trading houses and operated fur and Indian trading posts throughout the mountain area.

[41]Carlos Beaubien and Guadalupe Miranda were the original owners of the Mexican land grant popularly called the Maxwell Land Grant. Beaubien was part of the Bent-St. Vrain trading group and a member of the American community in Taos. Maxwell, the Bents and Carson were also members of this group. General Kearny had been in command of the United States forces that seized New Mexico in 1846. He was aided in many ways by the Bents, St. Vrains, Maxwell, Carson and other Americans living and working in New Mexico. Charles Bent became the first civil governor of New Mexico, but was assassinated in his Taos home during the abortive rebellion in 1847.

[42]Murdo McKenzie was manager of the far-flung Prairie Cattle Company in northern New Mexico and Colorado, and later had a hand in the Matador outfit. He was one of the most important of the British ranch managers in the day of the big cattle companies.

[43]Fort Lyons, near present Las Animas, Colorado, became the trading center of the Arkansas Valley in 1872 when the Kansas Pacific Railway extended its tracks to that point.

[44]There are many accounts—but no complete or analytical one—of the Maxwell Land Grant and its role in the history of southern Colorado and northern New Mexico. In addition to accounts in the general histories of these states the reader will find more detailed material on the Maxwell Grant in Harold Hathaway Dunham, *Government Handout* (Edwards Brothers, Ann Arbor, Mich., 1941), 212ff., and in Herbert O. Brayer, *William Blackmore: The Spanish-Mexican Land Grants of New Mexico and Colorado 1863-1878*, Bradford-Robinson Printing Co., Denver, Colorado, 1948.

Selective Index

149

154

Afterword

Marian Sloan Russell was among the vanguard of a small and select group of American pioneer women who came to know the Southwest in those wild and perilous decades before the arrival of the railroad brought about a rapid transformation of the land. Unlike the Oregon Trail, which bore legions of farm families to the Pacific Northwest, the Santa Fe Trail was a highway of commerce frequented mainly by merchants and private freight contractors. Women travelers and women settlers were few. Hence, their special role in the Trans-Mississippi West as preservers of gentility, education, and culture—the graces of living—assumed even larger importance.

Susan Shelby Magoffin, wife of trader Samuel Magoffin, tells us in her diary, initially published in 1926, that she was the first American woman to cross the prairies on the Santa Fe Trail. The journey, with wagons belonging to her husband, was made in the summer of 1846, fully a quarter-century after the formal opening of the trail in 1821. Her claim to being first remains unchallenged, since to date no record has appeared to suggest that any other American lady preceded her.

Native New Mexican women, however, seem to have traveled the trail in reverse, from Santa Fe to Missouri, with some frequency in the years prior to 1846. One of note was Dolores Perea who went east on a buying trip with her brother-in-law Antonio José Chávez during the spring of 1843. Their small and poorly defended party was held up by bandits in eastern Kansas, and Chávez was brutally murdered. Dolores Perea's

157

presence is confirmed by a single document in the federal court records, which shows that she gave an eyewitness account of the crime at the trial of the culprits in St. Louis.

Following Susan Magoffin's excursion to Santa Fe in 1846, which coincided with the United States' conquest of New Mexico at the beginning of the Mexican War, other American women found their way over the Santa Fe Trail. Some were female relations of merchants and of military officers posted to newly established forts in the Territory. A few were wives of Protestant missionaries. Bishop (later Archbishop) Jean Baptiste Lamy brought several contingents of nuns. And then there was a handful of typical pioneer women in slat-sided sunbonnets who with their families traveled the Santa Fe Trail on the first leg of a transcontinental trek to the settlements of California. From this migration, we have fewer than a dozen journals and memoirs kept by women participants, and most of those are disappointingly brief.

Unquestionably, the two best accounts, judging by quantity of detail and keenness of observation, are the ones by Susan Magoffin and Marian Sloan Russell. And, as the introductory note to the present volume affirms, it is Russell's that must be ranked first in picturing the human side of life on the trail. Her love of prairie travel and her fascination with the colorful and adventuresome people who, for a variety of motives, embarked on a wagon journey to Santa Fe, embue her reminiscences with a lyrical quality and create a song in prose that is a tribute to a vanished era.

Unlike Magoffin's diary, which has been widely read and often quoted by historians, Marian Russell's narrative has gone generally unnoticed, except by a few specialists in western history. But they have long recognized its sterling merits and its potential appeal to a wider audience. The manuscript, under the title "Memoirs of Marian Russell," was first published serially by the State Historical Society of Colorado in *The Colorado Magazine* between May 1943 and May 1944. Therein, the work is described as a joint production of Marian Russell and her daughter-in-law, Mrs. Hal Russell. Several years before her death, at age ninety-one, Marian began relating the story of her life to Mrs. Hal Russell, who wrote it down, presumably did a bit of editing, and then submitted each page to her mother-in-law for criticism and revision. It appears likely that Marian Russell intended only to leave a record for her many descendants. Yet the opening lines of her first chapter, which express a desire that "these memoirs may help preserve to posterity the truth and the warmth of an unforgettable period in American history," suggest that she may also have had a larger readership in mind.

In 1954, the Branding Iron Press brought out a handsomely designed edition of Marian's memoirs, limited to 750 copies. A new title, *The Land of Enchantment*, had been added, some changes in the original text were made (by Mrs. Hal Russell), and two different photos replaced those that had been used by *The Colorado Magazine*. Very quickly the book went out of print, and copies today are difficult to come by. The present reprint represents a fascimile of the scarce Branding Iron Press edition, with the addition of this afterword and several newly discovered photographs.

In the two earlier printings, Mrs. Hal Russell is inadequately identified. That serious omission should be corrected here. Her maiden name was Winnie McGuire. According to her own statement, she was the first Anglo child born in what is now Yuma County, Colorado, in the year 1886. Daughter of a homesteader who struggled to make a go of it in Colorado's harsh eastern prairies, she grew up loving the wide and sunlit land on one of America's last farming frontiers.

In 1904, Winnie McGuire earned a teacher's certificate and for the next twenty years taught in Colorado and Wyoming schools. In 1923 she met and married Hal Russell, who had a varied career as a hunting guide, government trapper, and stock raiser, and who in 1911 had helped establish the Brazil Land, Cattle and Packing Company in South America. Winnie went to live on the Russell family ranch in Las Animas County, west of Trinidad. Her own father had traversed the Oregon Trail as a boy in 1844, and later, while following the Santa Fe Trail, he had been chased by Indians in the vicinity of Fort Union. Perhaps the recollection of his experiences prompted her to take an interest in Marian Russell's story and to encourage her mother-in-law to get it down on paper.

In addition to her collaboration on *The Land of Enchantment,* Mrs. Hal Russell published in 1956 a fetching little book called *Settler Mac and the Charmed Quarter-Section,* recounting the hardship and family warmth of her childhood days on the prairies. She also wrote several magazine articles and prepared a history of Las Animas County for the State Historical Society of Colorado. Hal Russell died in 1966, and Winnie in 1970.

One section of Marian Russell's memoirs is disappointingly short, that dealing with the killing of her husband Richard D. Russell during the flare-up of trouble over the Maxwell Land Grant in 1888. She herself evidently did not understand the complexities of the case—indeed, few people did at the time— and in her account she confesses to not knowing why Richard became spokesman for the anti-grant faction. A more compelling reason for her brevity can be found in Marian's own sorrowful words. To write of Richard's tragic death, she tells us, "is not to tear open an old wound for the wound has never healed." The circumstances surrounding his violent end were so painful, even as she dictated her story at age ninety, that Marian Russell felt constrained to pass over them rapidly.

Readers of the present volume who wish to learn more about the land problems that led to the taking of Richard Russell's life may consult Morris F. Taylor's excellent study, *O. P. McMains and the Maxwell Land Grant Confict* (University of Arizona Press, 1979). Taylor devotes special attention to the shooting of Russell and to its effect upon settlers on the grant.

Of her older brother, William Hill Sloan, who shared many of her early trail experiences, Marian Russell provides only sketchy biographical details. To these, a few bits of information can be added. William was born September 4, 1843, at Fort Washita, Indian Territory, where presumably his father, a military surgeon, was stationed. The Russells, mother, son, and daughter, were in Kansas City between trail excursions when Will enlisted, July 19, 1864, as a private in Company A, 17th Kansas Volunteer Infantry. He received a warm send-off upon marching away to fight in the Civil War. But Marian observes that smiles would have been less in evidence had she and her mother known that they would not see Will again for fifty long years.

Before his enlistment, William had worked briefly for the *Kansas City Journal,* and military records show his occupation as "printer." But religion was his true calling, as Marian notes, and while employed by the *Journal,* he studied for the ministry on the side. Following his war service, William entered the Rochester (New York) Theological Seminary, a Baptist-supported institution. He completed his studies in 1873, having received bachelor's and master's degrees. During his tenure as a student, he married (July 14, 1870) Ida Augusta Preston, by whom he had eight children.

At varying intervals, William served Baptist pastorates in the eastern United States. In 1875, he went to Rangoon, Burma, where for three years he acted as superintendent of the American Baptist Mission Press. During that period, he also wrote and published *Practical Method with the Burmese Language.* Subsequently, he undertook two missionary stints in Mexico, the first from 1884 to 1888 and the second, 1893 to 1907. Some time after the later date, as Marian mentions in passing, he left the Baptist Church and became a convert to Catholicism.

In 1911, William took up residence in Las Cruces, New Mexico, which, if not precisely the end of the Santa Fe Trail, was at least within the Territory where he and sister Marian had gained so many happy childhood memories. Two years later when he wrote to the Military Pension Department in Washington, D.C., his letterhead showed his residence as Riverside Ranch, Las Cruces, and listed his occupation as editor and proprietor of a religious publication, *La Bandera Católica.* The letter asked for an increase in his pension, from fifteen to eighteen dollars per month, to which he was entitled because he had reached his seventieth birthday. "The Lord knows I need it," he told the government's Chief Clerk.

Failing health may have prompted William Sloan to go to Fort Leavenworth, Kansas, for treatment in the military hospital. At least we know that an army physician, Lt. Fletcher Taylor, attended him there and certified, on William's passing, April 26, 1917, that the cause of death was "organic heart disease." Burial was at the National Military Home in Leavenworth, not far from the place where William, Marian, and

161

their mother had departed in 1852 with the caravan of Francis X. Aubry on their first adventure to Santa Fe.

About the later life of Marian's mother, Pennsylvania-born Eliza St. Clair Sloan, little is known. The Los Angeles, California *City Directory* shows her a resident of that city in the years 1890 to 1892. She evidently made several trips to visit the Russell Ranch in Colorado; one record places her in Trinidad during the summer of 1894. Marian, neglecting to mention the date, says only that she died in California.

For reasons difficult to determine, the two previous printings of the Russell memoirs misspelled Marian's name. Surviving family papers as well as her tombstone give the correct spelling, Marion. To remain consistent with the foregoing text, I have continued to use "Marian" in this afterword.

If one believes the evidence incorporated in the writings of many early-day travelers, the Santa Fe Trail was an enchanted road leading to an enchanted land. It seems to have possessed, inexplicably, a near-mystical quality that drew people to it and transformed them. Marian Russell avers that the trail became her point of outlook upon the universe, and the blue vault of sky above it, bread and meat for the soul. "If you have ever followed the old trail over mountains, through forests, felt the sting of cold, the oppression of heat, the drench of rains and the fury of winds in an old covered wagon," she says confidently, "you will know what I mean."

Except for a few grass-filled ruts lingering upon stray patches of undisturbed prairie, the Santa Fe Trail that Marian Russell knew is no more. But in her recollections, there is preserved for all time the faint echo of rumbling wheels pushing southwest toward the promised land of New Mexico. And in them is recorded a faithful picture of a proud, resourceful, intelligent, sensitive woman who was as authentic a pioneer as America ever produced.

An impartial reading of these memoirs demonstrates that Marian Russell was an open and honest person, singularly free of prejudice against ethnic minorities. When she says that "Indians were bad along the Santa Fe Trail," meaning "hostile," she spoke from experience. But her words do not imply a personal belief—one then all too common on the frontier—

that the Indian was an inveterate enemy devoid of redeeming qualities. Likewise, throughout her book, Marian makes clear that she had a strong liking and natural sympathy for New Mexico's Hispanic people and their culture. As did her fellow countrymen of the day, she refers to native residents of the Territory as "Mexicans," which is technically an error, since from the end of the Mexican War in 1848 onward, they were American citizens. Marian Russell's opinions, to which any writer is entitled, were exclusively her own. Reprinting of her volume suggests no agreement or disagreement with her views on the part of the present publishers. It is offered in simple recognition that perspectives of yesterday provide valuable insights in interpreting today's attitudes toward social progress.

Thanks are owed to Eleanor Marion Stringfellow of Cañon City, Colorado for extending permission to issue this new edition of her grandmother's book. Her granddaughter, Noreen I. Stringfellow of Pueblo, Colorado, who is collecting Russell family records, also gave valuable assistance in the preparation of this volume.

Mrs. Viola Russell, who still lives (1980) on the old Russell Ranch in the Las Animas Valley and is the last living daughter-in-law of Marian, provided me much useful information. She also directed me to the little cemetery high on a pine-clad mesa above Colorado's Eden-like Stonewall Valley. There Marian Sloan Russell, who died on Christmas Day, 1936, from injuries suffered in an automobile accident, lies buried next to her gallant soldier. She herself had helped select the site in 1876 for this diminutive burying ground in what she described as the wildest and most beautiful place around. Her own best epitaph can be found in the final paragraph of her book: "My heart had returned to the land the old trail ran through, so long ago."

Marc Simmons